*Vision and form
in the poetry of Albert Verwey
1865–1937*

Vision and Form in the poetry of ALBERT VERWEY

Poems from the *Oorspronkelijk Dichtwerk*
with renderings in English verse

THEODOOR WEEVERS

THE ATHLONE PRESS
LONDON

First published in Great Britain 1986
by The Athlone Press
44 Bedford Row, London WC1R 4LY

Copyright © Introduction, English translations
Theodoor Weevers 1986
Copyright © Dutch text, Mr Gerlof Verwey 1986

British Library Cataloguing in Publication Data
Verwey, Albert
Vision and form in the poetry of Albert Verwey, 1865–1937 : an anthology of poems from the Oorspronkelijk Dichtwerk with renderings in English verse, preceded by an introduction, a concise biography and four studies on aspects of Verwey's poetry.
I. Title   II. Weevers, Theodoor
839.3'15   PT5875

ISBN 0–485–11296–5

Library of Congress Cataloging-in-Publication Data

Weevers, Theodoor, 1904–
Vision and form in the poetry of Albert Verwey.

English and Dutch.
Bibliography: p.
Includes index.
1. Verwey, Albert, 1865–1937 — Criticism and interpretation. 2. Verwey, Albert, 1865–1937 — Translations, English. I. Verwey, Albert, 1865–1937. Oorspronkelijk dichtwerk.   II. Title.
PT5875.Z5W43 1986 839.3'1162   85–16321
ISBN 0–485–11296–5

Typesetting by TJB Photosetting Ltd, South Witham, Lincolnshire
Printed in Great Britain at the University Press, Cambridge

In loving remembrance of my Sybil

I wish to express my gratitude to the Kitty van Vloten Stichting, to the Stichting Dr Hendrik Muller's Vaderlandsch Fonds and to the Stichting Van den Berch van Heemstede for their financial support which has made possible the publication of this book.

Contents

Part I

Part I

I Introduction

Albert Verwey was a poet of exceptional integrity and resilience. His life ran an even course and was, on the whole, a happy one. But few poets can have had such an eventful life from the artistic point of view.

His was an early, almost meteoric rise[1]. His first major work, the short epic poem 'Persephone', was swiftly thrown on paper at the age of 17. Shortly before, he had encountered the poet Willem Kloos, six years his senior, who discovered, guided and admired him, and fairly launched him on what promised to be a career of poetic achievement and success. The circle of like-minded young authors and artists who soon gathered round the two friends gave to both their unstinted admiration and support. But the halcyon days were of short duration. Verwey's engagement and subsequent marriage were a shock that turned Kloos, almost overnight, into a malicious enemy of his former close friend. The shock was mutual: Kloos' sudden hostility turned Verwey away from almost uncritical admiration and passionate devotion to a mood of profound self-analysis and self-questioning – apparent in his long poem 'Cor Cordium' – which presently compelled him to revise his mode of expression utterly and permanently. After some years of doubts and poetic experiments his wholly new poetic approach met with hostile criticism, first by Kloos, then by others. Verwey's popularity vanished suddenly, never to return.

In the course of some ten years he achieved a new style; he completed volumes of distinct promise, followed by several of mature beauty – only to see them abominated and decried as uninspired, over-intellectual and laboured. He persevered, nevertheless, on his determined course. He succeeded, by dint of a marked power of persuasion and organisation, in gathering round his new periodical several of his former associates and many promising younger talents. He encountered the great German poet Stefan George, who proved both an admir-

ing friend and a support through his like-minded fight for the
new poetry in Germany. Some ten years of felicitous leader-
ship followed. But once again fortune turned against Verwey.
George, developing into a powerful, almost overbearing
leader of men, gradually built up an educational, artistic and
political community on autocratic lines, which Verwey found
himself compelled to oppose and combat. So this friendship
also cooled and almost withered. Nevertheless his influence on
the course of Dutch life and letters continued unabated. But by
1918 the effects of the First World War had ruined the financial
foundation of Verwey's third and most influential periodical,
De Beweging, and with it most of his contacts with men of letters. He stood alone once more.

This crisis, too, was overcome by a poetic self-communing
that resulted in even greater achievements. Then, in 1924, the
appointment of Verwey to the Chair of Dutch Literature at
Leiden inaugurated ten years of teaching, during which, again,
a band of younger scholars and poets assembled round him. It
was terminated in 1935, his seventieth year.

Meanwhile, Nazism had arisen in Germany and become
dominant with Hitler's election as Chancellor in 1933, and a
similar, imitative movement was beginning to find adherents
in the Netherlands. For the last time the ageing poet, once
more rising to the challenge, marshalled all his intellectual and
poetic powers in order to resist this menace to humanity. In
several poems and two outspoken lectures he fought it and
exposed the prevailing apathy. When in 1937 he suddenly died
of heart failure, he was honoured as the national leader of stature he had once more proved to be. His inspiring example
proved a force for national solidarity during the German occupation.

This passionate, dedicated life is reflected and in many cases
portrayed in poetry outstanding both by its profound thought
and its perfection of form. Not unlike Goethe, whom he
resembled in personality but not socially, he has left a work
which could likewise be described as 'fragments of a great confession' – but with the important rider that nearly all the poems
are too entirely un-selfconscious to be, in the true sense, a
poetic autobiography. The fascination of his poetry lies, fund-
amentally, in the fact that Verwey, in poem after poem,

answered each challenge he encountered, whether personal, poetic, moral or political, and rose above it either victoriously or with acceptance.

In spite of undeniable unevenness, his *Oorspronkelijk Dichtwerk* (1938, 2 vols) contains many poems that will abide through their consummate artistry. But beyond that it offers to those who also seek religious and moral enlightenment the unique spectacle of a personal and poetic life – the two cannot be separated – inspired and illumined by a never faltering striving for integrity in action and expression. It was in the full awareness of this aspect of his work that the poet wrote the final stanza of the introductory poem to his last volume:[1]

What can I do for everyone
But urge them: follow my life's course:
Not for my sake, but since I know
That straightening the tangled ways
Gives wanderers peace. Be welcome then,
You, young or old, woman or man.

II Albert Verwey in his time
– a short biography[1]

Albert Verwey (1865–1937) was born at Amsterdam in the period that saw the swift development of Holland from an almost static agrarian and seafaring nation into a rising commercial and industrial one. His father, the owner-director of a cabinet joinery, was a serious-minded man with a poetic bent – a number of his poems in manuscript were preserved by his sons – who belonged to a fervent group of Dutch Calvinists. With his equally devout wife, he brought up their children, of whom Albert was the eldest, in a living faith which, greatly transformed, ultimately became the foundation of the poet's mature work. Both parents died young, the mother when Albert was 5, the father when he was 13 years old. The son developed swiftly. Already in early adolescence he found himself unable to subscribe to the dogmas of the orthodox Reformed Church. At 16, he decided not to be confirmed, and his stepmother and grandparents reluctantly agreed, following the express injunction: 'If he should prove different from us, then leave him free' which was found in his late father's will.

His intellectual development was equally rapid. Having successfully attended the five-year secondary school, gaining high marks especially in English, he was, at the age of 17, appointed first clerk, then secretary to the directors of a prominent Amsterdam business concern with extensive possessions in the pioneer West of the United States. In 1883 he was selected to be their secretary-interpreter when they decided to travel to Cimarron in New Mexico in order to assert control over their American deputy Frank Sherwin, who was developing dictatorial tendencies. This thrilling voyage across the Atlantic, then by train and horse-drawn coach via New York and Chicago to Cimarron – where, the mission completed, Verwey fell dangerously ill, was nursed back to health by a pioneer Dutchman, and 'experienced the landscape, with its distant snowpeaks, with unforgettable acuteness' – saw him returning a mature young man, and its profound impressions stimulated his imagination, as is evident from several poems of a much later date (Epilogue to 'The Crystal Twig'; 'The White Sail', Part II, pp.124, 188).

Well before the American voyage, Albert had already begun to write verses, at first in the manner then current in Holland, but soon branching out into greater emotional and artistic freedom, stimulated by the English poets read at school whom he had begun to translate and freely to imitate: Byron, Coleridge, Wordsworth and above all Shelley, 'the soul of fire', who, along with Keats' *Hyperion* and Shakespeare's Sonnets, proved formative and lasting influences.

It was a year before the voyage that he first met the student of classics and poet Willem Kloos (1859–1938), his senior by six years. Verwey decided to study literature at the university, which necessitated sitting the 'Staatsexamen' in Latin and Greek, and had begun to study on his own – a tall order for an unguided school-leaver. Kloos, who immediately discerned the promise hidden in his young friend's first poetic efforts, soon became his mentor, not only in the study of the classics, but in the art of poetry. His generous friendship, and the constructive but no less unsparing criticism of Verwey's poems, soon led to a mutually passionate friendship which inspired Verwey's sonnets later published under the title *Van de liefde die vriendschap heet (Of the love named friendship)*[2] (see Part II, pp.94–99) and several sonnets by Kloos. Being aware both of their radical departure from current poetic practice and of the hostile reaction to their own poetry, they began to co-operate closely in the fight to 'make room' for the new poetry by critical essays in the few periodicals willing to accept them, in which they propounded views, revolutionary in their age and country, which were a more outspoken development of Wordsworth's preface to the *Lyrical Ballads*. They were soon joined by Frederik van Eeden, L. van Deyssel and, somewhat later, by the painter-poet Jacobus van Looy, Herman Gorter, who was to become the originator of Dutch impressionist poetry and free verse, and the poetess Henriette Roland Holst (*née* Van der Schalk). This was the group of authors who later came to be known as the 'Beweging van Tachtig' (the Movement of the 1880s). This movement, in which Verwey took a prominent part, was markedly influenced by the English Romantic poets, and to a lesser extent by the French Symbolists. It reacted strongly against the romantic nationalism and the homely but rather pedestrian poetry on conventional domestic and religious themes current in Holland at the time. In their critical essays, for which they presently founded the periodical *De Nieuwe Gids* (1885), Kloos, Verwey, Van Eeden and Van Deyssel (then a great admirer of Zola), demanded expressiveness of rhythm and originality of metaphor and diction, and propounded the maxim 'form and content in poetry are one and inseparable'. Their poetry, like that of the pioneer who preceded them, their elder contemporary Jacques Perk (1860–81), Kloos' friend, who died before the latter encountered Verwey, struck an entirely new note. Whereas Potgieter, the great poet of the Romantic period (1808–75), was a patriotic castigator of his country who never ceased advocating emulation of Vondel and Hooft, the poets of the Dutch Renaissance, they worshipped the beauty of nature, above all nature as the image of the beloved and the mirror of self; they deified the self, which was godlike in its depths (Kloos). Above all, along with their English and French contemporaries, they worshipped beauty, with the devout feelings of a believer kneeling before his god. Ideal beauty, which they found in Shelley and Keats especially, was the aim, which was realised in Kloos' best sonnets, in Verwey's sonnets and his epic poem 'Persephone'[3]. The movement's greatest achievement was Gorter's lyrical epic *Mei*. The latter two poems were, clearly, influenced by Keats' *Hyperion*, with overtones from *Endymion*.

The friendship of Kloos and Verwey – which in the former showed a homophile tendency, while Verwey's ecstatic admiration in *Of the Love named Friendship* was inspired and in part modelled on Shakespeare's sonnets – was disturbed and very soon shattered by the impact on Kloos of Verwey's engagement and subsequent marriage to Kitty van Vloten. Kloos experienced a complete nervous breakdown then. He came to hate the 'unfaithful friend', while Verwey, deeply shocked as he was, showed himself consistently compassionate and loyal, maintaining a balanced, if critical regard for his friend and erstwhile mentor, and a generous recognition of the greatness of his early work.

Verwey's marriage was a happy one. Kitty van Vloten, who from their first encounter, and throughout their long life together, took a lively and understanding interest in Verwey's poetry, was his never-failing support, also socially, for although their home in the then undeveloped dune-village of Noordwijk – a lively environment with their happy, increasing family (three sons and four daughters) – was essentially homely and never assumed the 'allure' of a 'salon littéraire', their Villa Nova (called 'Dünenhaus' by Stefan George) was always a hospitable centre, where many of the poet's Dutch and German friends loved to stay and to exchange thoughts on the art of poetry. Gorter, Jac. van Looy, L. van Deyssel, Henriette Roland Holst, and later Alex Gutteling, Maurits Uyldert, P.N. van Eyck, Jacques Bloem, Aart van der Leeuw, the poets of the *Blätter für die Kunst*, especially Verwey's friend, rival and ultimate antagonist, Stefan George, enjoyed the stimulating poetic friendship of their host.

Ist ein dach noch das so tiefen friedens
Freien stolzes neben solcher fülle –
    Düster-mütigen starren gast
Lud und hielt und fern oft winkte?[4]

The crisis of broken friendship left its mark on Verwey. It was only after several years of intensive reading and reflection (Vondel and Hooft, Shelley, Goethe, Spinoza) that he, at first with somewhat rugged determination, but soon in *De Nieuwe Tuin* (*The New Garden*, 1898) achieving mastery of his authentic form, began to write the monumental, organically harmonious work, by which he gradually found a measure of recognition with the élite among his country's poets, critics and artists – as well as a good deal of persistent misunderstanding, which was to a considerable extent due to Kloos' malicious decrying of his 'intellectualism and Calvinist moralising'.

Verwey was a strong personality of exceptional stature and integrity. His influence as a critic proved a powerful force in the change from exuberant impressionism (of which Gorter's 'sen-

sitieve verzen' were the outstanding, and influential summit)
to the harmonious expression of matured imaginative concep-
tions that became the main trend of the period extending
(roughly) from 1900 to 1920. Verwey exerted this influence
through the periodicals *Het Tweemaandelijksch Tijdschrift* (1894–
1902) and *De Twintigste Eeuw* (1902–5) which he edited jointly
with Van Deyssel, and, as sole editor-in-chief, through *De
Beweging* (1905–19), for which it was the ambition of young
poets to get their poems accepted, since they had come to
regard this as an honour and a symbol of recognition.

Among the circle of regular contributors Verwey found a
number of admiring friends. Some of these became close
friends, especially Alex Gutteling (1884–1910), whom he
regarded as his disciple and spiritual son, and Maurits Uyldert,
who remained a staunch supporter, and wrote the poet's biography in three volumes (1948, 1955, 1959). Others were P.N.
van Eyck, a poet akin to Verwey in some respects, who was his
successor to the chair of Dutch literature in the University of
Leiden; Aart van der Leeuw, a poet of the 'Earthly Paradise';
the poet-novelist Nine van der Schaaf, Jacques Bloem, a
blood-brother of Leopardi; Hilde Telschow, the translator of
his essays on major European poets (*Europäische Aufsätze*, Insel
Verlag, 1919). By far his most gifted friend was Stefan George,
outstanding among his German translators, along with Rudolf
Pannwitz. His closest friend was the great Dutch painter Floris
Verstér (1861–1926).

From 1924 till 1935 Verwey was professor of Dutch literature
in the University of Leiden. Here his gift of educating and
guiding young people found fresh scope. The success of his
teaching showed in many theses in the field of Dutch literature
published in that decade; its imponderable impact still continues to be felt through his one-time students' work and
teaching.

During the last five years of his life Verwey saw the rise of
Nazism and the ascendancy of Hitler and his henchmen in Germany. He felt it deeply, and answered its challenge strongly
and openly, not only in two public lectures, *Het lijden aan de tijd*
(The suffering caused by this age) and *Onze taak in de tijd* (Our
task in this age), but in a number of outspoken, indignant
poems, such as 'De dichter en het Derde Rijk' (The poet and
the Third Reich), 'Aan een vriend die wil dat ik vrede predik'

(To a friend who wishes me to preach peace), and in the Cantata for students '*Honestum petimus usque*'.

In these final years Verwey was a national personality of widely recognised stature, and even beyond his lifetime he remained an influence towards national solidarity under the German occupation.

The greatness of Verwey's mature work lies in part in the fact that it unites several apparently disparate qualities: a strong spontaneous intensity in the short lyric, a marked power of contemplative reflection and a never weakening urge to build complex poetic patterns of harmonious form. His tendency towards dramatic presentation is seen thoughout the work, and culminates in three Goethean dramas of ideas, *Johan van Oldenbarnevelt*, *Jacoba van Beieren* and *Cola Rienzi*. These plays have been found both impressive and stageworthy when performed; they would deserve to be produced more often than the inevitably restricted stage of a small country can by its very nature achieve.

In the present transition from complexes of separate national states to the ultimately hoped-for universal community of mankind, Verwey was and remains a liberating force. Against his influential friend and adversary Stefan George, he championed the cause of international fraternity, both privately and in some poems; he consistently urged it during the First World War, and it was the mainspring of his fight against 'the closers of frontiers' on the eve of the Second World War. Verwey was both a patriot and a convinced believer in the inevitable development of mankind into a universal community. As a poet he felt a member of the brotherhood of poets of all nations and ages – an individual voice in the chorus of singers in whatever tongue was theirs. 'Every language is suited for the poetry of those who speak it,' was one of his sayings. He was equally sure that true poetry is the expression of 'the love that moves the sun and the other stars' – the love that animates all the generous impulses of man.

He was a great and versatile translator, as he showed in his *Poëzie in Europa*, a collection of translated lyrics by major poets from Petrarch onwards and from Italy to Finland, and his verse translations of Shelley's *Alastor*, Dante's *Divina Commedia*, of Shakespeare's sonnets, Marlowe's *Doctor Faustus* and Milton's *Paradise Lost*, of which he completed the version begun by Gutteling. He was also a cultured traveller, and visited New Mexico, France, England, Spain (as witness his sequence of sonnets *Spaanse Reis*), Italy, Sweden, Finland, and especially Germany, where Stefan George was often his host, first at Bingen, and later in Berlin and Munich.

III Vocation: the idea of poet-hood

Among European poets since the Renaissance Albert Verwey stands out as one of the great personalities. Few poets – one thinks of Goethe, the young Wordsworth, Shelley, Stefan George – have been so conscious and so convinced of their poetic vocation, or so aware of the eternal value of poetry for mankind. Verwey voiced this conviction on several occasions. In the Preface to the first volume of his *Proza* (1920) he wrote: 'The Idea of Poetry is of importance not only for poets. It is that creative power of imagination which is certainly embodied most completely in poetic works, but which, as the first and foremost human urge, coincides with life itself. Everyone experiences moments in which he is a poet.' The poet's office was, so he wrote on another occasion, 'the highest form of spiritual life'.

These views are undoubtedly a further development of those voiced by Shelley in *A Defence of Poetry*, which was admired and translated by Verwey. They can be seen to have become the basic tenets of his criticism. He recognised in Shelley's ideas the expression of a feeling which had already found utterance in some of his own early poems written before Shelley's *Defence* had become known to him. It is important to realise that this intuitive feeling was there before he saw it confirmed and brilliantly formulated by Shelley. The origin of Verwey's conviction, that poetry is the living heart of mankind and is inherent in every human being, lay in his poetic experience. He was a poet before he developed his ideas on the nature of poetry. In his militant prose he was, throughout life, a 'defender of poetry'. He *experienced* poetry as a vocation. To that vocation he devoted his life, and his poetry can be seen as the infinitely varied expression of his awareness of the cardinal importance of poetry for the spiritual health of mankind.

The essence of poetry remains the same through the ages,

however greatly its forms may and do change. In every age there were poets whose utterance determined their form, and others whose sense of form was so strong that it lent to all their utterances an unmistakable emphasis, cadence and tone. It goes without saying that there is hardly any poet with whom utterance and form do not appear simultaneously and inextricably; but mostly one is dominant. With the former – I mention Wordsworth, Heine, Verlaine, Whitman – utterance is so spontaneous that it *creates* its form, whether apparently traditional or new. Poets of the latter kind – Milton, Mallarmé, Stefan George – are by their very nature destined to express themselves in an inborn form as permanent and unmistakable as their voice; their personal verse, their stanza are already there before their utterance even begins to unfold.

One need only see this contrast clearly to realise that the former tendency – for the utterance to mould its form – has been dominant since the last war, and this has usually, though not necessarily, caused a loosening of form. The question whether Verwey is a poet of the former or of the latter type cannot be gone into, however, until the dilemma has been considered more closely. In this matter the word 'form' is, after all, ambiguous. It can denote the aggregate of verse and stanza forms, including free verse, used by the poet in question. Form, however, can equally well be used for the poet's 'inner form', the characteristic feature of all his utterances that is the audible aspect of his personality as it is voiced in his work. If the latter meaning of the term is intended, the dilemma ceases to exist. With any true poet conception and expression, sound and thought, are so wholly *one* that the question of the priority of either cannot even arise. One could quote almost any poet to confirm this. Verwey wrote, in 'The Song of Recognition':

> More than sense and mind
> As though born before the utterance
> Lives in us that Form, that inner Kind,

in which 'inner Kind' is a rendering of 'ziele-leest', i.e. 'shape of soul'.

One can legitimately inquire, however, into the preponderance of either utterance or *prosodic* form. There are, doubtless, poets – Stefan George is outstanding in this respect – with whom the personal verse forms dominate and, almost subconsciously, mould the utterance, whereas with others – Wordsworth is a clear case – the utterance is sovereign, and its rhythm, with all its self-willed irregularities, shapes the highly individual verse. In a manuscript note (which I quoted in *Droom en Beeld* (p. 167) Verwey comments with evident admiration: 'One can hardly translate Wordsworth unless with freedom in syntax and diction, because that freedom is the preponderant feeling, *which one must share if one is to translate him at all!'* (my italics). Since Verwey did translate a number of Wordsworth's lyrics and long passages from *The Prelude*, one has to conclude, which is in fact borne out by many of his poems, that with him, as with Wordsworth, the utterance, with its spontaneous rhythm, is there before its prosodic form, whether metrical or free, has been established. The integral rhythm of the utterance is paramount.

This inner necessity of absolute integrity is one of Verwey's fundamental qualities. It compelled him, around 1887, to reject radically the style and spirit of what he had so far published and, literally, to start from scratch – to 'stammer', as he was to call it later. He was well aware that, in doing so, he threw away the very possibility of ever being a 'popular' poet. With steady perseverance he pursued his course until he had developed his own form. Approximately between 1888 and 1898 this development was completed. But he fully retained that spontaneity which caused him to renew himself afresh again and again. He was able to do so because his inborn nakedness of utterance immediately showed the slightest change of emotional or intellectual disposition. His utterance absolutely conforms to the conception. Where the conception required it, his tone and style could be harmoniously flowing, or subtle, or graceful. In the opposite case, tone and diction, even the rhythm, could become harsh and rugged, even cacophonous.

This nakedness of utterance could be called his personal style; but the style was not an adopted one. It was an inner necessity: on each occasion he could not have expressed himself otherwise. When the conception is irrational, his utterance accords with it. Not through the quasi-profundity that can be suggested by symbolistic haziness or by synaesthesia; his diction remains as exact, the sentence-structure as clear as in other poems. Yet such a poem can be obscure; but its obscurity arises from the conception, the mysteriousness of which is conveyed, unretouched, in imagery that is sometimes bewilderingly enigmatic, as in the following passage:

In the bloodclot-lumpy soil
Where the rusting metal of burnt-out shells
Splinters in uprooted furrows,
Are there seeds swelling?

Wrecks still darken the ocean-floor,
Hanging 'mid waters,
Ruins stand leaning in the fields,
Burnt and broken,
But far on the gleaming face of the sea – are those fleets
Full of nourishing cargoes?
Yonder on the desolate field, are those puny figures
Steering the ploughshare glistening in fertile furrows?
I sit in darkness.
Shapes are still moving faintly as if on waving screens.
Where is the heart of the world, that I, its knower,
Safely may dwell there and shelter and hear it beating,
May neither lament nor ask, but as a trustworthy
Seer may unriddle the future?

This is the opening passage of 'The Two-sided Shield',[1] a poem written shortly after the First World War. I am not now concerned to attempt an elucidation of this very profound poem, in which the poet arrives at a reconciliation of his awareness of being at the mercy of dark irrational forces and his reliance on the light of the conscious mind. What I want to point out is that here the impulses arise immediately in the subconscious, and that they, as it were, *condense* into words in that borderland between the unconscious and clear consciousness, where rational thought is powerless.

Verwey here 'switches off' his conscious will and listens to what arises within him. The essential quality of this poem is that reality appears in it so changed as to become unrecognisable, almost like a nightmare. What is the cause of this and what does it signify? The Russian poet Boris Pasternak, in his essay *Safe Conduct* surprisingly accounts for such apparent distortions of reality.

> In all art we experience the conception more directly than anything else. We no longer recognise reality. It appears to us in a new form. This form seems to us an inherent feature of reality, not of us. Apart from that everything that exists has its name. That feature alone is new and nameless. We try to give it a name – and the result is a work of art... Through the poet's feeling, reality has been shifted. Art, like a telescope, is directed on to that reality and it registers the shift. The work of art is a portrayal of reality *as it appears to the artist.*[2]

It seems to me that this applies in a literal sense to those poems by Verwey which are most congenial to us at the present time. I have in mind a poem such as the following:

May Day

How near by,
How like then
Gleams the copse and shines the fen,
Rings the skylark that with song commands the sky.

Full of cares
Forth I went,
Ere I knew came Spring and sent
My eyes agaze with greenery, full of sound my ears.

Who stayed young?
Who grew old?
Spring came, smiled ... and *my* heart sang
Anew the very tones she will to a youth unfold.

The poet is overwhelmed. He has gone out, he sees and hears – and the world is suddenly new, transformed. His feeling *will* find utterance, and all it does is, in humble simplicity, to say in a few words what he sees and hears and feels. It is a recognition of an experience of youth. Once, also *then*, the copse was so

near, so gleaming, did the skylark's song so fill the air. Is he
seeing the landscape? no, he *is* the landscape – green, his eyes
are swelling with green, his ears are full of bird-song. And in
expressing that smiling sense of spring his heart sang the
triumphant song which creates its own symbolic form: this
unusual stanza, which from a couplet of short lines three times
rises into a broad hymn of triumph: the symmetric form of a
harmonious utterance.

We must now consider more closely the view, still held by
some, that Verwey is a 'cerebral' poet. That view originates in
a misapprehension due to the reader's realisation that some of
Verwey's poems set him thinking – which is a fact. It all
depends how this is done.

Until it finds utterance, thought tends to be confused or cap-
ricious. But once the average person sets himself to write
down what he is thinking, he first realises his whole sequence
of thoughts and then writes it down as an ordered *train of
thought*. The average person is seldom able to do that in verse.
But supposing he managed it, the result would in fact be cerebral, although, by its very nature, not poetry; cerebral poetry
is, indeed, attempted sometimes, but, in my view, it is a precarious borderline phenomenon rarely brought off successfully.

Verwey's poetic thought is a totally different thing. He
hardly thinks – he muses, 'dreams' or meditates. And this
mode of thinking develops in a continuous interplay with
what his senses perceive. Whilst looking and listening he meditates, and this meditation finds utterance in words inwardly
spoken while meditating, in the rhythm of spontaneous breathing. It *grows* from association to association, and that is how
a poem arises through which there runs no discursive train of
thought, but a stream of spontaneous associations. But let us
leave the poet to say it. In a poem of 1924 we find the following
rhymeless stanza:

How marvellously what's in the heart will grow!
One can dig up a plant with flower and foliage
And root, and, with the dew still on its leaves,
– If handling it with care – transplant it
In other soil; – it can be touched by hand,

Its bodily form remains then as before –
But that a thought should be transplanted from
Our mind, in words communicated,
That is a marvel. He of whom I spoke
Did even more. What he transferred in words
Was far more than a thought, was its arising,
Its sprouting, branching out, its culminating
In bud and flower. From a dark tiny seed
It blossomed and still wears its dew of stillness.[3]

The poet of whom Verwey here speaks is, I am convinced, Wordsworth; he evidently felt akin to him.

This poem cannot be said to be *of* a certain period. This speaking is timeless. It comes from that mode of being where everything is both new and familiar, where plant life is spiritual life and where the human form is seen as soul. In that mode of being the poet has lived in moments of grace. One such moment is recorded in the volume *The New Garden*. It is both one of the loveliest and the most enigmatic I know. I translate, as closely as possible:

Did not an ear thus swell in fields, my heart,
That grew of sun and sap till from thin green
The golden corn-head in its hairy beard
Sweetly arose, to meet the winds' warm kiss?
Swelled not the blue until the sun-head grew
Black with its blazing and engulfing glow?
Gleamed not, a dusky girl whose beauty gleamed
Darkly, the earth, as pearls in water do?
Swelled not our body so, which, like a field,
Its dewy heart laid open to the sun?
Swelled there not gold into ripe rounded gleam?
Glowed not the light coal-black that's plumbed by none,
Dark mystery of an engulfing dream
In which light blazed where white the body spun?

One can indeed analyse the imagery up to a certain point. There is a correspondence between the swelling ear of corn, the blazing 'sun-head', and 'our body' – the three parallel mysteries which together, and inseparably, form the poet's dark secret dream. But beyond that, rational analysis is helpless here. One can, it is true, attempt to penetrate the poem by means of a psycho-analytical interpretation, but then one almost of necessity violates the hermetic imagery by reducing it to psycho-analytical symbols, thus robbing the images of their originality; and in the end one thereby at most explains an aspect of the poet's mind, but not the poem. Undoubtedly its imagery has a sexual component. In stating this one merely says that, as a mystery, it is akin to another, equally fathomless mystery. Rilke once wrote: 'Und tatsächlich liegt ja künstlerisches Erleben so unglaublich nahe am Geschlechtlichen, an seiner Weh und seiner Lust, dass die beiden Erscheinungen eigentlich nur verschiedene Formen einer und derselben Sehnsucht und Seligkeit sind.'[4] He spoke clearly and yet said no more than can be stated in rational language.

The expression in this poem is strikingly full and almost velvety in sound, almost tangible-making and yet tender in its touch. Whoever has tried to arrive at an appreciation of the nature of Verwey's sound-symbolism soon realises that this is a gigantic undertaking, because his expression is so astonishingly diverse. Take ten successful poems on ten wholly diverse subjects and you will find ten radically different forms of sound-expression. This phenomenon is due to Verwey's characteristic form of spontaneity. He does not consciously adopt a different point of view, nor does he intend to produce a different effect; he suddenly *is* different; again and again he experiences life differently, almost as a different being. He obeys this impulse, he surrenders to that feeling; hence his utterance really becomes the utterance of a different man. Naturally this is not the case in all his poems. No poet is always wholly inspired. It is certainly possible to find poems written in what one might call Verwey's characteristic manner. But these are not his best. And it is surely a recognised truth that a poet is only truly known from his best work.

There is one more reason why Verwey on occasion will express himself so wholly otherwise that the reader will look up in astonishment. That is because he had, to an unusual degree, the gift of identifying himself with another person, so much so that, for the duration of one poem, he as it were *became* that person. He was aware of it; as he once said to Stefan

George: "What I love becomes part of me. I incorporate it."[5]
Time and again this happened to him. All George's 'herrscher-liche' personality is embodied in Verwey's second poem on the death of George, 'Bij de dood van een vriend' II, where George's spirit answers his friend, who had called him 'free at last':

I have not willed such freedom. I desired
To be a god; I knew of no existence
Beyond my own. The Other – that was merely
The chaos, unillumined by my light.
I dwell now not in higher spheres, but lower,
Spectre-like, bloodless. What remains of me
In sunlight on your fair earth is the work
Of mine in word and deed, the everlasting
Bearers of my indwelling form, which the later
Living revere, imprinted in their minds,
Binding all that's divided ...
                When I, wholly
Un-bodied, soulless roam through the immense
Abysses of the universe, I know your earth
Is mine: my being: all those dwelling there
Are of my offspring, and I laugh and rule.[6]

Whoever, on reading this, might imagine Verwey to have been of a similar type, a natural ruler of men, would be mistaken. He consistently disapproved of this side of George's bearing and openly showed his radically different attitude. It was alien to him. But in this poem he *was* George. Whenever, through this entire identification, Verwey voiced the utterance of another person he was, so to speak, temporarily transformed to his very lungs and vocal cords, he *was* that other person, for the time being. This experience of being identified with another or others was once described by him in the poem 'De Levende' (The Living One). There, on seeing an excited crowd,

O, I felt as if caught in black hair,
In its meshes entangled, afraid,
And yet wishing to be with *them*,

But then I sat still, for a need
Came, stronger than joy or pain.
In my thoughts I was with *them*,
At heart I would always be
With the crowd that I know within
In each sound, each gesture I see.
But the seeing was strong like being,
I felt bound to what inwardly formed,
It grew in me, seemed my doing,
Myself, in whom weird things stormed.
And I lingered, sat on in the dark
While the blaze and sound died away …
What was that ringing, that spark
Brought into me, come to stay …
I sat in a wide, still room,
But walls I saw not, none –
A sea full of flakes of foam,
A sky of sorrow and moan –
A world where I was adrift,
Where I ruled and drew blissful breath –
An abyss – o how I lived –
A darkness – o beauty of death.
…
My lonely day is again
Round me: I see them all go
Once more, those figures; I learn
Each inwardly to know.
In my thoughts I am with them,
At heart I shall always be
Where the throng moves – I know it within,
In each sound, each gesture I see.[7]

This is the dramatic aspect of Verwey, an essential element of
his poetry. The dramatic poet is 'objective' – in Verwey's term,
'impersonal', no matter who speaks through him. Even when,
viewing superficially, one might believe that he himself was
speaking. For this 'self', through the power of poetry, was
divested of its subjective quality, its egotism, and it was conveyed objectively. The poet then saw, portrayed and expressed
'himself' exactly as though it had been another person. This

dramatised self which is no longer a personal self constitutes the mythical Poet, who is the protagonist in Verwey's poetic work. The dramatic identification with other people led to countless portraits, to be found in all the volumes and, naturally, it is the driving force in Verwey's dramas.

Verwey is a maker of images in the true sense of the word; he creates them because they arise within him; he does not invent them. He has such complete confidence in the power that manifests itself through his writing, that he will receive the image and allow it to unfold, even though he does not yet know what it is going to reveal to him. Sometimes this remains a mystery, at least for the reader. Whenever – which is often the case with Verwey – a poem in its entirety is one image which impresses the reader as having a profound significance, whilst at the same time remaining so enigmatic that not a single interpretation can satisfy us entirely, we may call it a *myth*.

I will not attempt a discussion here of what constitutes a myth, a problem that has been considered from several angles. One cannot help noting that even a scholar such as C. S. Lewis[8] did not attempt to give a definition although he did state a number of characteristics of *myth* as he understands the term, which is the sense in which I propose to use it here. Among these the following stand out:

(a) Even at a first hearing it is felt to be inevitable;

(b) The characters are like shapes moving in another world;

(c) We feel indeed that the pattern of their movements has a profound relevance to our own life, but we do not imaginatively transport ourselves into theirs;

(d) The experience is not only grave but awe-inspiring. We feel it to be numinous;

(e) Certain stories which are not myths in the anthropological sense, having been invented by individuals in fully civilised periods, have what I should call the 'mythical quality'. [Lewis mentions Kafka's *The Castle* as one instance.]

Some of Verwey's mythical poems are re-creations of traditional myths, others are original. But a feature of both categories is what Lewis finally observes. 'And after all allegories (of the myth) have been tried, the myth itself continues to feel more important than they.' One may try one's hardest to give an allegorising interpretation of a mythical poem; but in the end one can do no more than attempt to approach a mystery inaccessible to reason with rational means. One never gets beyond a rough approximation. And that is as it should be. For it is the challenging enigma of a mythical poem that forms its greatest fascination.

Verwey's mythical poems are numerous. They are not entirely disconnected. As was first observed by Maurits Uyldert and after him by Van Eyck and others, his poetry as a whole embodies one myth: the myth of poet-hood (Dichterschap). For although it originated in the life-experience of one person, that experience and that person have been re-created by the objectifying imagination of a poet who, through inner necessity, saw all he experienced in the light of eternity. He felt as if there was a unique mirror within him – in one poem he even saw himself as 'De spiegel zelf' (The mirror itself). It follows that his poetic work is not an autobiography in verse; nor is it, in Goethe's sense, 'fragments of one great confession'. For it is impersonal and – strange paradox – a self-portrayal devoid of egotism. It is the monument of a life integrated in poetry.

That the strictly mythical poems form part of the one all-embracing myth of poet-hood is evidenced by the connection between them – a non-rational connection, but demonstrable by the associative affinity of their imagery. Certain images: that the poet is the builder of a city, on the 'mountain' of which he erects a cathedral in honour of his Lord; a king who reigns in a world created by his imagination, through which there runs an eternal river, will recur from time to time, never identical and yet unmistakably related. They appear to be detached, and are, in fact, but there is felt to be a connection.

Occasionally we find a mythical poem that has almost all the aspects of this myth. I mention one, 'The Beggar'. Of this strange story it is eminently true that no interpretation can 'explain' its mystery.

It is a dialogue between two persons, a 'he' and a 'she', who in the end prove to be two aspects of the poet. The opening lines are spoken by 'him':

Into that very stillness
We have returned
In which, long since, our dwelling in this land began.

At that time he feared that a relapse into his former turbulent
city-life could disturb this new life and work.

Now my anxiety is different: I've achieved
What then I dreamed:
My life now is a city I have built
With its approaches, gateways; the broad streets
Lead into squares; parks overshadow
The eternal stream; my mountain rises high and steep
And from its sloping sides I see the world,
The boundless one, in which a blessed people
Dwell in the houses, move around and work.
But on the mountain did I build my highest house,
My great cathedral, statue of my Lord.
How shall I go, now I have climbed to there,
And knelt,
How shall I go towards my loved ones yonder,
To all the thoughts I had in younger days?
Or must we, you and I, alone, on yonder side
Tread downward slopes
Knowing that also there a world awaits us?
It is the country of the setting sun
That now is stretching, building-less and broad.

The word 'building-less' is significant. The city, the people
who live there, the cathedral – all this is the realm of the imagination of which the poet is the maker and the king. The summit has been reached. Must he, the player of 'the lyre that fits
and orders stones', together with her, his inspiration, who
'bears the lamp of the burning heart' – must he descend, leaving the mountain of his sublime dream, and erect new buildings on the downward slopes that lead to Night?
Then, at last, She speaks:

You will far sooner stay upon your mountain
And, like Elijah, on a fiery chariot
Be taken hence.

But She knows better what is right for him. After all, he does
not desire regal eminence above the world of men. He is a king
who wishes to serve his people and to walk unrecognised
among them:

You're one of those who even in Heaven
Would not forever dwell, but you prefer
The turbid world, humiliation,
Renunciation of the glory you have won,
The marriage with all life: humanity.

'Do not detach yourself from your people,' she goes on to say.
'For as soon as you leave their community, their whole existence will become unreal.'

I breathed more deeply as she ceased,
And turned about.

Now he knows what he should do. He will stay in community
with the people created by him, he will dwell among those yet
to be created; and he will receive back from them the life he
gave them:

The bells were ringing as I, unobserved,
Mixed with the throng. I wore a beggar's cape,
Held out my hand and, without looking –
For each strode swiftly to his work – each gave
The gift I'd once conferred on him.
I all along grew stronger, seeing each glad face,
And recognised by no one. In the market-place
I sat down by the spring and thought: Live on, my people,
I am the unseen bond through which you are,
And in your buildings I'm the humble mortar,
The sound that rings from all your bells –
I'm the receiver of your charity:
Give, give!

And like the drops which always from their fountain
Rose and fell, just so was over me
From day to day, their giving.
To me, their beggar,
Everyone gave; henceforth none knew his city
Without its beggar.
And no one realised he was the king.

At the risk of appearing to regard the poem as an allegory, I have, in my account of the passages that had to be left out, attempted to elucidate what might otherwise remain obscure. But the poem is far from being an allegory. Its essence is the myth of poet-hood, and its symbolism allows of more than one interpretation.

As a myth of the poet's function, the poem is profound. The (unrecognised) king builds the city of this dream; but through his city runs the river of eternity, which is beyond his power. He is both ruler and beggar; creator of men, he is at the same time, as portrayer of those he encounters, limited by their individualities. He reigns and serves; he builds, and yet can only build on the level ground of his life which, as old age approaches, extends downwards towards the sunset that must be followed by Night. He is free and tied, mighty and has to submit. His rise and fall are as fixed and inevitable as the revolving motion of the earth. The earlier mythical poem, 'Zijn drie gedaanten' (His three embodiments) is so profound as to defy analysis.

There remains a difficult problem, which I will not evade. How are we to understand the word *idea*, as some critics have used it when considering what they termed Verwey's Idea? The poet himself used it only rarely, once in his Preface to the *Verzamelde Gedichten* (1911/12), and in a relatively small number of early poems. Later on he avoided it.

The word is almost doomed to be misunderstood. It is only with difficulty that one can detach oneself from the current international usage, in which it has come to mean 'notion', or even 'fancy'. However, if we return to its original Platonic sense of 'form', 'shape', we can indeed apply it to Verwey. For is not the form of his work the myth of poet-hood? In other words, its 'idea' could only be conveyed in and through that myth. That it could not, in the customary sense, be 'put into words', surely goes without saying; the poet himself never ventured to attempt it.

I do indeed believe that some of the poems are eminently *central*, in that they convey the core of the central mystery more than others. No objective criterion for this can be found. One reader will prefer one particular poem, another a different one; and even with the same reader this preference may well vary in the course of years. We will consider two poems here in this light. The former is as follows:

> I opened wide my arms, believing
> I was embracing thee, sheer light,
> When, leaning to my cheek, a grieving
> And tearful human face I met.
>
> And from my dazed lips words were dropping,
> My words of comfort, in her hair,
> And, pulses with compassion throbbing,
> I felt her arms, how limp they were.
>
> Moved unto love by her affliction,
> Forgetting wish and work and thee,
> I found, bewildered with compassion,
> Her burden light, not hard the way
>
> Into my garden, to my dwelling,
> And there she stood; I beckoned: Come –
> Bright splendour blazed; home shone, a temple,
> When thou didst to thy sanctum come.

He who wanted to embrace life's mystery, Love, found in his arms the earthly beloved, and as he led her into their joint home, Love itself made its entry there. Not in this poem alone, but evermore afresh did Verwey embody this central experience in a poem, always through an image. This is the one pole of the mystery. What predominates here is the yearning of love which, aiming as it does at the light of love itself, finds its realisation through and in the love for a human being.

The opposite pole is the direct contact with eternal Love.

The poet experiences it in those moments when the inspiring force within him speaks so clearly that his listening to that inner voice comes to his consciousness as listening to a living being he loves. In the poem 'The One' this being is for him a regal lady whom he both protects and worships. He is her knight – but not an infatuated Knight of La Mancha. For his adoration is not given to a mortal, but to the Beloved Lady, who so wholly speaks within him that he cannot really distinguish her voice from his own.

The One

I always with my very body
Have shielded you, and those who see my bearing
Know not what I am like for you.
So harsh and cruel do the rampart walls
Rise up enclosing the secure Alhambra:
Fountain and gardens and the cooler hall.

I have worn out my strength through that protection,
I have defied the hatred of all men,
I have refined my mind into the web
Of stratagems that make not me
But you unwoundable.

You are the fairest, truest, dearest one.
My virtue merely lies in that I love you.
All those who know you not, will taunt me, asking:
'Art such another knight from that La Mancha?' – Truly,
I answer not: 'And yet Dulcinea is the fairest.'
No maiden from Tolosa is my idol-dream.

There's no reality to equal you,
Fountain of life! Who knows my restlesssness
Must know that only then does it exist
When my eye meets not yours. And yet – your eyes,
My sorceress, where do I see them not?
They smile from heaven and they are on earth
In living beings, happenings, and at night
They sparkle in my sleep.

There's nothing that avails me but your nearness.
But most your speaking. For I often wonder
As I hear myself whisper, if it is not you
Who whisper then.
This is the sweetest converse, when I know not
If you and I are two or one. I listen,
And as I listen soul weds unto soul.

How rich your thoughts are! During all my years
I would hear other ones, which yet were clearly
Coming from you. – Still there's this mystery
That you have voiced your thoughts, since time began,
Through many men. When in myself you're silent,
I read those once recorded by your own.

How right was he who spoke: 'Whoever sees you
And loves you not, has no idea of love.'
Also: 'her loveliness is new to earth
Because it was from elsewhere she received it.'[9]
From elsewhere. – No, I seek you not on high.
Heavens too are old. But you *are* in the eternal
Elsewhere that is the pole and origin of Here.
You are Newness itself, that's born within us.
You are the Joy at heart of all earth's pain.

By no means disagreeing did I hear that fierce
Condemner, the Charontian
Foe of all rosy viewing:
'Earth is a hell.'[10]
'Within that hell's a heaven' was my whisper – warding off
His fell indictment? No, confirming it.
Amid this hell, delusion, this our world,
And ground of its necessity, there is You!

Hail to all those who know you, only good and true and fair
And real one.
They have within the hell their stronghold firm
Of blessed peace.
And Noah's dove that with the olive branch
Did skim the Flood and reached the Ark

Was not as scatheless
As they are, resting in the abyss. If ever
In the mad chaos of this age, my courage
Once faltered, if I ever, for one moment,
Believed that all the cunning, the bad faith,
The greed and power-lust of a ruthless gang
Could ever overwhelm you, strike me then,
Deprive me of your presence, hurl me down
Out of my core of peace. But I do know –

I know another mystery.
O my tremendous winged one,
It is your storm-flight that once caused the welkin's layers
To shift, and everywhere brought down
Bewildering confusion, ere you lighted.
I know your nestling on the wave, I know
In you the stirless balance of tranquillity.
Forgive me what just now I said.
Could *I* protect you?
You spread your wings all over me: I shelter,
I am a nestling in your warming down.

An interpretation of this poem will not be attempted here. I leave it to speak for itself. One feels it is central and that it constitutes the opposite pole to the poem quoted before. There, one who saw clearly beheld in the mutual love of two mortals the radiance of eternal Love. Here the poet speaks to the creative power within him which the Ancients called the Muse, whom he knows to be the supra-personal form of love which acts through poets. For him she is so truly a living Beloved that he hears her voice and sees the light of her eyes.

In this poem there speaks a faith in life that was undefeatable, because it had passed through the world experienced as hell, and in that fire was not destroyed but steeled. It is the faith in the oneness of human and divine love which forms the axis round which this infernal world, our erroneously believed reality, circles. He who, with his 'Praying Youth' felt himself to be standing 'as the tranquil axis of that dome', found amidst the distractingly revolving universe his pole of peace.

IV Organic structure

If, after close reading of the individual poems of a volume, one awaits the integration of one's impressions, so as to survey them in their entirety, one will find that, as a single whole, they convey an atmosphere that proves lasting – indeed, one feels like a traveller who for a time has lived in a world resembling ours, and yet different. Thereupon the reading of the opening poem of the next volume comes almost as a shock. The poet's imaginative bearing, and hence also ours, has suddenly changed.

In this way each of Verwey's volumes – he liked to term them 'books' – has its own recognisable, unique physiognomy. Sometimes the poet is aware of sojourning in an unusual world, as in the opening passage of *The Bright Universe:*

> This is a mellow world, in which the light
> Dissolved in mist will reach my cell
> And grows in denseness round me; and I dwell
> In this white universe as a sailor may
> Live quite alone on a forgotten island –

This is a feature which Verwey shares with other poets. With them, too, one observes how every volume of poems has its own atmosphere, often contrasting with that of the preceding one. However, his poetry has a further characteristic feature which is found in the work of only a few poets. His poems certainly have their own individual character; but beyond this they evince a demonstrable cohesion, an interrelation, and they even adumbrate a development which it is hard to define but which nevertheless makes itself felt as one comes to know any of his volumes as a whole. His poems are, in fact, interdependent – not in the sense that they embody a train of *thought* – but rather a 'train of feeling', in which each poem has its place, like the links in a chain, so that their order cannot be altered. Their ordered sequence is part of the essence of Verwey's poetry.

Naturally this cannot be perceived until one has become familiar with, at any rate, several volumes. Whoever reads any of Verwey's books for the first time can, of course, only experience each poem by itself. It is not until one can survey and analyse one of the larger units *as a sequence* that one begins to sense vaguely, then perceive more distinctly, that the volume is a book with a definite structure. Structure such as this, however, can be the result of two very different, even opposite modes of creation. It is instructive and enlightening in this as in other respects, to compare Verwey's work with that of Stefan George. With George, a volume of poetry likewise embodies a train of thought or feeling and a development; but this arises – as can be verified from several of George's utterances on the subject – from intense thought during the period of conception but *preceding* the actual composition of the work as a whole. The poems then represent an admirably sustained and developing conception, but their order is not necessarily a chronological one: it is a structure due to deliberate composition.

In Verwey's case, the poems do not merely arise spontaneously, they are in no way premeditated; their sequence *unfolds* in the manner of organic growth. Their order is chronological; as the sequence gradually comes into being the poet is still unaware of any development. It is only when the entire completed volume lies before him that, with amazement, he perceives that they express, or rather symbolise, a hitherto subconscious emotional or spiritual growth. The connection is hardly ever an intellectual one. What links the poems is nearly always irrational; it may be that the dominant images are akin, or that the motifs of the poems are related either through similarity or through polar interdependence. This connection would, always afresh, strike Verwey himself as little short of miraculous. The poems, again and again, would occur to him spontaneously, as the result of an experience or an encounter, they were genuine 'Gelegenheitsgedichte' in the Goethean sense; but they proved to be links in a chain, and their order was a necessity, from which he could not deviate, even when – as he sometimes did – he might wish to arrange them arbitrarily according to a momentary impulse. How entirely he was then made to realise that there was a power within him which he could not rebel against, is well brought out by the following poem, again quoted in my translation:

The Instrument

Strange musician, who hast bound me
To an orbit past my conscious mind,
So that soon or late when Time's revolved around me
All my keys lie open to thy hand,

Outside thee not one chord can be sounded,
Not a chord will sound but must perforce
As a direct sequel be expounded,
One with all the others in their course.

Powerless am I, and not just to say,
But to order, by caprice or skill.
Never can I break the lifelong lay
Which thou once began through me and carry on at will.

Ruthless one! I sometimes thought to escape thee,
To be free and, as we humans please,
Roaming here and there in aimless dreaming
To enjoy my peace.

Fool I was! – for, as I searched, meandered
Vainly, and with ever lessening strength,
Hoping I myself might steel my powers,
And escape thy might at length,

Came thy urge that like a harp-string strained me,
And a cry broke from me suddenly,
As once more thy spirit tamed and claimed me
To serve thee.

This interdependence of the poems and the consequent necessity of maintaining their chronological sequence was seen by Verwey himself to be due to an innate form of polarity. In an essay of his later years he wrote:

> The realisation, indeed the discovery that I had *always* expressed a polarity in my work, almost forced me into a mode of thought and vision in which this should be impossible, in which all duality should be integrated in one conception. [...] The entire book *Het Eigen Rijk* was the outcome of this experience. But this work was no sooner completed than the need to communicate the insight I had gained caused me to write the next volume: *Het Rijk in de Wereld*. Inner life and external reality had once more proved to be each others' polar opposites, and I could only experience their fundamental one-ness in the poem *Nieuw-jaarsmorgen*[1] an imagined dream-world in which inner life and outward reality are shown as mutually symbolic of each other.[2]

The significance of this profound passage for the understanding of Verwey's poetry is unmistakable. Polarity was the fundamental structure of Verwey's poetic creation, and hence the basic feature of its form. His poetic expression was, inevitably, determined by it; he could only have avoided it by refraining from utterance.

V Verwey and Wordsworth

The growth of the poetic imagination

Throughout his career as a poet, Albert Verwey took a profound interest in the nature and function of the poetic imagination and its growth. When, in 1924, at the age of 59, he was appointed Professor of Dutch Literature at Leyden, his inaugural lecture[1] was entirely devoted to this subject. He traced the origin of the concept of Imagination and its development by philosophers and poets. He showed that, for Spinoza, it was still an inferior faculty nearer to what Coleridge later termed 'fancy'; that Vico in his *Scienza Nuova* (1725; 1744) first recognised it as an independent cognitive power; and that Jean Paul in his *Vorschule der Aesthetik* (1804) drew a clear distinction between the inferior faculty which he called 'Einbildungskraft' and the fundamental power which he named 'Phantasie'. This was the distinction which Coleridge adopted, using his now generally accepted terms 'fancy' and 'imagination'. We know that he shared and discussed his discovery with Wordsworth, for whom it became the central point of his poetic thought, and indeed the theme of his great poem *The Prelude*. So far Verwey. I have reason to believe that in his view, Wordsworth treated the very subject with which we are concerned. *The Prelude* is known to have been embarked on as a spiritual autobiography addressed to Coleridge. As he proceeded, Wordsworth became more and more concerned with what eventually was to be the sub-title of the poem as it was published posthumously: 'Growth of a Poet's Mind'. In other words, the subject of *The Prelude* was the development of *one* poet's mind, Wordsworth's. But he realised that much in this development was common to many poets, and indeed true of the growth of the human mind. In *The Recluse* which, along with *The Prelude*, was to have been part of that much vaster poem which Wordsworth never completed, he wrote:

Not Chaos, not
The darkest pit of lowest Erebus,
Nor aught of blinder vacancy, scooped out
By help of dreams – can breed such fear and awe
As fall upon us often when we look
Into our Minds, into the Mind of Man –
My haunt and the main region of my song.

Now Verwey, who, as we saw, was akin to Wordsworth and knew his work well, in the years immediately before 1920 – the year in which the poems were written with which we are concerned – had been making a close study of *The Prelude* with the intention of writing a full-scale book on it which owing to circumstances was never written; but significantly, his notes and sketches centre round Wordsworth's thoughts on the nature of the imagination. He had also more than once written broadly autobiographical poems similar to *The Prelude* in manner and approach, though of far more modest dimensions. But, during a fortnight of July and August 1920, he wrote the cycle of twelve twelve-line poems that forms our subject: *De Legenden van de Ene Weg* (The Legends of the One Way). This is a work of an entirely different order. It is not a narrative poem at all. Each poem is separate, terse, wholly devoid of argument; each treats one scene or concept apparently disconnected from the others. One can indeed perceive connexions and even development, but these remain implicit.

Clearly, the form of Verwey's 'Legends' has nothing in common with that of *The Prelude*. Indeed I know of nothing comparable in Wordsworth, for in such cycles as 'The River Duddon' the connexion is wholly explicit, quite apart from the fact that it consists of sonnets. But Verwey's cycle does call to mind the form of another poet with whom he had an affinity, Stefan George, his German friend, rival and antagonist. George's cycle *Der Teppich des Lebens* consists of twenty-four poems, each of four quatrains, whereas Verwey's 'The Legends of the One Way' is a cycle of twelve poems of four tercets each. Formally, therefore, the two cycles are akin if not identical; but they differ in approach and content. Enigmatic as *Der Teppich des Lebens* will always remain, it can be seen to suggest a development which is cultural rather than psychological and spiritual. 'Der Teppich' is the tapestry of life and art. It unrolls a veritable configuration of vividly portrayed people from succeeding periods of history: peasants, knights and ladies, monks, pilgrims, asocial wanderers, even criminals – then artists, poets, and finally seven symbolic statues embodying aspects of art. Each is a nameless, sharply outlined personality representing an aspect of past life or art. George's central concern is the development of life and art in succeeding periods 'as these live in him', and constitute aspects of his art. His art has the power both of evoking past life and of awakening yearning for it. He will make it spring to life, and even step out of the framework of the tapestry:

> Da eines abends wird das werk lebendig.
> Da regen schauernd sich die toten äste,
> Die wesen eng von strich und kreis umspannet,
> Und treten klar vor die geknüpften quäste,
> Die lösung bringend über die ihr sannet!

This is part of the opening poem which evokes the overall tapestry of which each of the following pictures then forms part. We shall see that Verwey's cycle is the realisation of a widely different conception. He also, it is true, will be seen to suggest a development embodied in a succession of images. The nature of that development can be discussed better gradually, as we proceed to examine each poem. But one important difference is immediately apparent. The cycle straightway takes us 'in medias res'; it lacks an introductory poem suggesting an encompassing framework. Consequently, the images are not presented as flat pictures in a two-dimensional world. They are as it were suspended in space, and illumined by flashes of creative light. That suggestion of space is unmistakable in the first Legend:

The Constellation

> The way was narrow and the dale was dark,
> He knew that in the thickets snakes were hiding,
> The heavens were a thin and glimmering line.

He had gone down; he climbed now, slender, stark,
As though the boulders sped his upward striding,
His bludgeon, firmly gripped, a trunk of vine.

And when it seemed, up on the highest rim,
As though eyes burning bored into his eyes,
– He raised his weapon for the monster's charge –

He saw, inclining towards him from the skies,
The constellation winding, and its golden cords,
A labyrinth of light, enfolded him.

In its spare, austere form, two separate sestets, each consisting
of two tercets, whose lines in the original rhyme in the order
a b c a b c: d e f d e f, the poem evokes an image of primitive life.
Primitive man, alone in his puny weakness, bravely faces the
unfathomed mysteries of the universe, which he feels to be
menacing. It is an image of primitive life, indeed, an image of
primitive imaginative life. This man faces, not a cave-bear or
mammoth such as we find depicted in prehistoric drawings,
but a constellation of stars which his imagination views as a
monster; and his weapon is a trunk of vine, traditionally the
poet's emblem. He is a primitive poet, if only a subconscious
and potential one. As such he belongs to the distant past, but
also to the present, since individual man retraces the development of the race not only before birth but also in childhood and
adolescence. This imaginative savage, this adolescent poet, is
gripped by numinous awe before the grandeur of stellar space.
Being wholly inexperienced spiritually, he feels threatened by
an unknown force, which his imagination visualises as an
immense monster with staring eyes. He prepares for a desperate fight against the luminous giant. But ... the monstrous
force proves benign: it enfolds him in its splendour and merci-
fully spares him the hopeless struggle against supernatural
might. Man's individual will, though ready to resist, is encompassed in the Will of the Universe.

There is no doubt that both this poem and the three succeeding ones embody a stage of the human imagination which is
not merely primitive but definitely animistic. The imaginary
danger faced here is felt to be a monster. In the next three

poems a rock, a mountain ridge, a tree are likewise pictured as creatures animated by living forces dwelling within them.

The White Sail

The rock-face closed. Like espaliers of roses
Arose the mountains, high, immensely far;
The land lay in a net of sun-sparks sunken.

He, coming from deep darkness, wavering pauses, –
Roaring of rivers, bird-song everywhere,
The sound and light making him still and drunken.

From underground existence he'd arisen
To be a dweller in this garden-sphere
And knew not how; nor where to make his way.

Then where the stream cut through the far-away
Mountains, he saw along a harbour-pier
A small ship with its white sail brightly glisten.

This, the second legend, is another image of primitive life. It always reminds me of that wonderful statue by Rodin, 'L'âge d'airain', a slender male figure lightly touching his forehead in half-dazed wonder as undreamt possibilities dawn before his mind. Like him, this wordless poet stands overwhelmed by the beauty of the radiant landscape that bursts upon him as he emerges from the ancestral cave. But this time man is not single-mindedly fighting off the mystery, he is reduced to wavering indecision, paralysed by rapture. Then his trance is broken by the sight of the white sail: a sign of the enterprise and the co-operation of man with his fellows. Society, even if primitive, now enters the field of the imagination.

The next poem is a scene of sheer horror. It evokes the terrors of barbarous society dominated by tribal superstition and magic rites.

The Bridge

They braved the raging stream to found their bridge.
But so that peace and strength should fill the stone:
'Whose love shall come here first, let's brick her in!'

The sun grew burning on hillside and ridge –
Singing she came who would reward her man
With rich-stored basket and a full canteen.

They lifted her – his arms were hanging limp, –
They placed her in the space, on purpose open,
They mortared, mortared, and aghast she gazed.

She screamed – this jest of men was growing grim! –
He stood dumb –, in her heart perished the hoping:
They mortared, mortared till the pillar closed.

This ghastly picture of the inhumanity of the age of barbarism is etched on the imagination by its starkly factual presentation. It goes back to a known source. Mr M. O'C. Walshe enabled me to follow up the suggestion made to me by Dr Mea Nijland-Verwey, the poet's daughter, that the subject was derived from a Yugoslav ballad. In this ballad (much too long and prolix to quote here)[2] a detailed description of the event is given and – possibly in an attempt to soften the barbarous theme for a more humane age – the wretched woman is not immured completely but allowed a little window through which to receive food and to suckle her infant. The sacrifice is demanded by an evil spirit who keeps on destroying the foundations of a building. The husband, however, never questions the necessity of the sacrifice. With Verwey, everything is cut down to bare, wholly tribalistic essentials. He thereby situated the event far back into an age which mercilessly and with absolute conviction relied on human sacrifice to ensure solidity of structure. There is no explicit comment. The stark factuality is never broken. Nevertheless the suggestion of evil is unmistakable. The poet's silence is a condemning silence – witness the contrast between the cacophonously voiced shout of the bricklayers – 'Wiens liefste 't eenst hier komt, metsel haar in!' – and the compassionate picture of the doomed wife: 'Singing she came who would reward her man/ With rich-stored basket and a full canteen.' In other words, here is the poet's implied condemnation of an age that believed in the magic rite of immolating life in order to ensure the success of the urge to build. We in fact witness man's self-will setting itself against

Life in order to realise its selfish ends by *any* means, however inhuman.

It is in the fourth poem, 'The Bird', that the oppressive earth-centred enclosedness of tribalism opens up to a sense of cosmic freedom. Two views of life are contrasted here.

The Bird

In the old tree the Dryad's whisper sighs.
A bird, blue-gold, settled among the leaves:
It came through the ether, from a strange far land.

'It lives through me, the Dryad, through my grace
The tree stays green. It dungeons me and leaves
Unheard my whispers in this prison penned.'

And the bird said: 'This morning as I journeyed
I passed the sun, and he sent out his rays
From star to star down to this youthful earth,

And where he shone, paradise-gardens burgeoned,
The creatures moved, bright flowers and plants arose:
By him alone were these green leaves called forth.'

If 'The Bridge' was the confrontation of closed minds with dumb yearnings of love, in which the earth-centred urges won, we witness here the clash of earth-centred, almost vegetative life with the growing imagination which for the first time opens up to the freedom of light and space. The Dryad embodies the short-sighted, self-centred mind which sees only its own efforts. She laments the tree's ungratefulness for what she regards as her own single-handed achievement. The bird, who has travelled through the sunlit spaces of the universe, knows that all life is engendered by the sun, that it is an un-merited gift to be received joyfully. All the Dryad's utterances are self-centred: 'through me', 'through my grace'. The bird voices an awareness of infinity; we sense the liberation of the mind from earth-bound superstition.

We are now in a position to see that the 'Legends' consist of a succession of six pairs of poems, and that each pair is linked by a form of polarity. The single-minded pioneer who fights the constellation finds his opposite pole in another pioneer whose open mind drinks in the beauty of the world. The inhuman builders immure a loving, outgoing wife; the self-centred Dryad rebels against the imprisonment that is inherent in her natural mission.

Now comes a momentous step in this gradual liberation of the imagination. In the fifth poem, 'The Departed', Man's mind conquers a new dimension. Henceforth he will no longer naïvely walk through an apparently endless stretch of timeless days. He now enters into the time-transcending communion with his ancestors and, in the sixth legend, also with the loved ones who will survive him. This mental conquest brings with it a new form of thought: meditation.

The Departed

We daily nurture with our blood the spirits
Of the departed, who in us live on:
They share in all we do and all we bear.

Their fight is ours and deep behind our cheer
Their still existence stands, comfort or scorn –
What our voice sings, their breath in us inspirits.

But they are blind. Our eyes are open, keen,
The universe within their gaze is ours,
We see the ways that lead from star to stars.

These ways are ours, and along these our course
Renders the raptures of their dream-weighed hours
For silent spirits sweeter and more serene.

Here the imagination of youth – both the youth of the individual and of mankind – truly grows up, and with maturity comes conscious poet-hood, the utterance in song.

At this point the primitive beliefs concerning intercourse with the dead and the modern conception of communion with them are merged. In the *Odyssey*, Odysseus is unable to hold converse with the dead in Hades until the spirits have drunk the blood of slaughtered animals.[3] Here the dead are felt to dwell within us, nurtured by our blood. That is a modern imaginative concept. The living blood in our bodies maintains the life of the departed who live on in our imagination, with that life of memory which Proust revealed in *A la recherche du temps perdu* (I am not suggesting 'influence' of Proust here, merely observing an affinity of thought which is not unique; Bisson has pointed to a similar experience in George Eliot in the first chapter of *The Mill on the Floss*.)

The growth of the imagination takes another big stride in the sixth legend, 'The Directed Will'. The poet's communion with past generations is established; he now discerns the link with posterity. And for the first time he speaks as an individual person.

The Directed Will

When I have died and those who loved me stand
Around my bier, when maybe one will ask:
'What did you love in him: his human-kindness,

His poet's gift, his faithfulness to friends,
The gentle strength that bears and shares distress,
The vision wherewith he fulfilled his task',

Then one, I hope, 'we know indeed' will answer,
'That as man, poet, friend, and as a guide,
A force, he did his part; but now that still

The wheel of thought stands and in self-surrender
His mouth has closed, we see his strongest might:
One aim, immortal Life, inspired his will.'

It is inherent in poetic maturity, as it is in maturity generally, that the mature poet is and feels distinct from his fellows and must, literally and figuratively, speak for himself. The poet of primitive tribal society represents the corporate personality of the tribe; he says 'We'; the modern poet, however deeply he may share imaginatively in the joys and sorrows of others, knows himself to be separate and distinct from them; he must speak in his own person. This is why the latter poems of the cycle are different in character. A Dutch critic, S. Vestdijk, regarded this as a flaw. In his opinion there was a rift some-where near the middle of the cycle. He went so far as to assert that at this point the poet had 'deviated from his intention of portraying the development of human thought in a series of mythological poems'[4]. This view to my mind had its origin in a double misconception. In the first place Verwey, as he indi-cated by his title, wrote 'legends' not necessarily on mytholog-ical subjects – in fact only one, 'Orpheus', is clearly based on a known myth. But moreover, he was, as we have seen, con-cerned not so much with the growth of thought as of the imagination. I would suggest that what appeared to Vestdijk to be a rift is in reality the inevitable transition from the approach of the primitive poet who voices the corporate personality of the tribe to the personal approach of the modern poet, who may and often does identify himself compassionately with others but nevertheless speaks as an individual person. That all the imaginative persons who appear or speak – anonymously – in these poems are of the spiritual, religious type, is clear. The as yet wordless poet who in 'The Constellation' faced the celestial monster was potentially religious: he was subcon-sciously aware of the Spirit of the Universe, and his resistance can be seen as a refusal to submit to an unacknowledged attrac-tion. Verwey is a poet of this type; and it is as a poet who voices the human imagination in its religious aspect that he speaks in those poems couched in the first person. Here, facing his own death and pondering on the image of him that will be remem-bered by future generations, the poet hopes they will recognise that his entire creative will was focused on immortality, 'op de onsterflijkheid' – that is, not on poetic immortality, lasting fame, as it was understood by Petrarch and the Renaissance poets, but on the fact that in his work he embodied those time-less moments of ecstasy that are in fact moments of eternity.

It is now clear that my initial formula, 'the growth of the poetic imagination', is rather too wide, since imagination in a general sense is not necessarily religious. In these poems it is, at first potentially, but then consciously so. They embody stages in the growth of that type of imagination, a growth which is a quest, at first a quest of something only dimly apprehended; but as the cycle unrolls it becomes a quest of the

ultimate power that inspires the poet. In the first four poems
the subconscious quest appears as a striving to conquer terrest-
rial space; it is with that aim that the pioneer in 'The Constellation' strides up the narrow valley, and that his counterpart in
the next poem is attracted by the white sail in the distance.
Even the inhuman bricklayers perform their nefarious rite in
order to safeguard the bridge which is to carry the road that
will extend their power on earth. But, unknown to all these
pioneers, there was in that horizontal drive for power an
upward striving towards the light – the light unwillingly faced
by the defier of the celestial monster, the light that dazzled the
pioneer emerging from his underground cave, and which was
hailed by the bird as the origin of all life. At this point that urge
becomes conscious. The poet Vondel, the protagonist in the
seventh legend, 'Maturity', who lost his wife in middle age, is
known to have felt the attraction of the poetess Maria Tes-
selschade, whom he sometimes addressed under the name
'Eusebia'.[5] Feeling himself to be on the verge of a passion that
would have drawn him back to the outgrown stage of young
manhood and thus destroyed the quest for the heights of
poetry to which he was now dedicated, he resolutely turned
away from this nascent love.

Maturity

'Eusebia, let go!' That cry from Vondel
As he forged onward with the firm decree
Henceforth to live alone and dedicated,

Having shed griefs' and pleasures' long-borne bundle,
So that his spirit, now entirely free,
Might win the clarity that liberated,

That cry is heard again where poets, older,
Mature, have known the world, and will pursue
Their chosen faith on visionary heights.

They feel how wings are growing from their shoulder,
Deaf to the weeping hearts that fain would sue
Them to enjoy once more the vale's delights.

Such a victory over self, such ruthless consistency is rare.
Immediately the pendulum swings back. The next legend
brings a sorrowful evocation of the mythical poet undone by
the great love which he strove to pursue and recover even
beyond death – Orpheus.

Orpheus

If Orpheus had not killed Eurydice
By wanting for himself her living eyes,
For ever he'd have raised her to the light.

Now he stood weeping where earth closed, and she
Had for all time withdrawn from his embrace
Whom he thought clasped unto his heart so tight.

Yearning alone remained, an open wound,
And his laments of downward-reaching longing,
Drooping and heavy, were like trees that mourn,

Whereas that Other One was once more bound
In the closed ring whence by his soaring singing
– Ah, for how brief a span! – she had been torn.

The thought is clear and profound: song perpetuates but yearning kills. The musical ecstasy of Orpheus could have per-
petuated his beloved in a timeless eternity of song; but his
yearning for her living eyes drew her down, away from his
embrace – once more to be that other Eurydice, the departed
spirit, and to complete the millennial cycle of which Virgil
speaks in the sixth book of the Aeneid: 'All these spirits, when
they have rolled time's wheel through a thousand years, are
summoned in vast throng to the river of Lethe, that, reft of
memory, they may revisit the dome above and conceive desire
to return again to the body'.[6] By their vowel harmonies the
verses underline the dichotomy of soaring song and drooping
yearning; thus 'in 't licht gevoerd' calls up the contrasting
rhyme: 'aan 't hart gesnoerd' – a vivid contrast between
spiritual exaltation and sensuous passion.

Poets, being human, may falter and fall, but the imagination of mankind continues in its upward striving. In the ninth poem, 'Soaring Strength', the poet speaks as the maker of a mountain lake in which his poetic power is stored. The water of inspiration is not permitted to flow freely towards the vale of earth; it is stored up in order that, lower down, it may spring up as a tall fountain, the droplets of which sparkle in the sunlight, beckoning the poet's soul towards the expanse of the sky. But the water then rains down on the flowers in the dell, and the poet himself joins in the thanksgiving of the birds and flowers, since, along with them, he receives the celestial gift which came through him but not from him. He rejoices in being both a child and a lord of the earth.

Soaring Strength

My strength, gathered into a level lake,
Shall not assuage the gardens in the valley
But only feed the fountain soaring high.

When with my eyes the mountain-range I seek,
The jets of water, starlike, seem to draw me,
Until in them I seem nearer the sky.

But as their droplets sprinkle down on earth
And flowers lift up their faces in the dell
And birds are twittering in the moistened bower,

Then, my heart full of what from heaven fell,
I feel both child and lord of joyous Earth
And listen to her thanks in which I share.

But again the pendulum swings back. In 'Soaring Strength' the poet's imagination was able momentarily to see water, like heavenly manna, descending on earth. He now re-experiences the tragedy of Eden – the first heaven-drenched garden – where God would walk with Adam and welcome Eve, until the desire to be as wise as God destroyed the original state of being God's children and banished Eve and Adam to a realm of rock and thorns, of misery and death.

Eve

When God himself would walk in Paradise
'I greet thee, daughter!' rang his hail to Eve.
How otherwise sounded the Serpent's strain!

'Thou shalt be like the Lord God, be as wise,
Not, trembling child, unto thy Maker cleave,
If of this fruit thou eatest, thy sweet gain,'

She ate. And Adam ate. The fiery sword
Drove both into a realm of rock and thorn:
Him who seemed godlike, and her, still a child.

Who grew to be a Mother and who bore
Abel and Cain, to death and sorrow born.
And God's voice rang no longer in the wild.

But once more, after this relapse – not merely a mythical
event in the distant past of mankind, but also the experience
of the loss of communion with God, an event of which the
human imagination cannot gauge the significance until it
has consciously experienced its separateness from God – the
upward urge resumes sway still more strongly. It now
becomes the mystical urge to approach the eternal light.
And this of necessity implies isolation from other men: the
distance between the poet and the rest of humanity
increases. This is symbolised as an ascent into the heavens.

Distance

Who rises sees earth's circle ever wider,
More amply ordered lands' and seas' expanse.
He knows his loved ones where they dwell and go.

He, liberated, beckons them as Liberator,
And in their hearts there wakens a new sense
Of order, seen on high, pursued below.

Below's the crowd, on high the boundless space,
But who attains that height draws each one's gaze,
A lodestar, focal point for every eye.

Then space descends, as though you did unlace
The knots and ties wherewith you hemmed your ways.
Distance ensues the word: – there you, here I.

One man, the poet, is here seen to ascend ever higher into the boundless space of infinity – and inevitably, while his achievement is admired as a distant triumph, the separation, the isolation from mankind steadily increases.

The closing poem takes us into a yet more rarefied atmosphere, where all is shadowless light except for the distantly viewed turmoil on earth.

The Ruler

Life is a beautiful and blood-stained war
Where each fights others for consummate power,
But greatest blessing is a steady rule.

I see wild turmoil spreading wide and far,
But in a wise Hand that shall judge and rule
Hangs moveless burning the predestined Hour.

The Ruler comes: his Peace does not bring death,
But drowns the unrighteousness of twofold life
In a new mode flawlessly pure and true.

He our First Origin re-openeth.
He ousts the phantom of twin natures' strife.
Creation's act by him is done anew.

The poem represents an essentially mystical vision which, being beyond sense, is necessarily unportrayable. One is aware of approaching it rather as the colour-blind must view the colours. But one thing is clear: far from being arrogant, the poet has here risen above his fallible self. Even so, he merely says: 'I see', the mystical Ruler whose coming he announces is not himself, nor any individual person, but the Absolute Poet beheld in this moment of vision. What this Absolute spiritual Ruler brings is the healing of the breach in the human mind that leads to the opposition of the individual will to the Will of the Universe. He restores the integral wholeness of the Imagination which is a feature of the ideal poet, but which can only be realised in flashes by individual poets. That perfect integral Imagination would enable man to perceive all experiences of sense as intimations of eternity.

This is where Verwey meets Wordsworth, the Wordsworth of *The Prelude*. The passage in Book XIV, line 188 (text of 1850) puts this beyond doubt:

> This spiritual love acts not nor can exist
> Without Imagination, which, in truth
> Is but another name for absolute power
> And clearest insight, amplitude of mind
> And Reason in her most exalted mood.

As Verwey demonstrated in the sketches for his planned book on *The Prelude*, Wordsworth equates *that* Imagination with Nature, and Nature, 'the speaking face of earth and heaven', was to Wordsworth the 'prime teacher of his mind', 'the Sovereign Intellect',

> Who through that bodily image hath diffused
> [...]
> A soul divine which we participate,[7]
> A deathless spirit.

And, as Verwey quoted with complete agreement in another jotting, that spirit is shared by inspired poets.[8]

> The power which all
> Acknowledge when thus moved, which Nature thus
> To bodily sense exhibits, is the express
> Resemblance of that glorious faculty
> That higher minds bear with them as their own.
> This is the very spirit in which they deal
> With the whole compass of the universe.

How completely Verwey understood Wordsworth's conception of the Imagination, and how entirely he shared it, is well
brought out by the following passage in his sketch on
Wordsworth, which evidently refers to the above passages. I
translate:

> The aim and object of man's existence is that, by living in
> community with Nature, he ever again establishes the
> divine Oneness which is his origin. The loss of that oneness
> is caused by the intellect and the senses, as soon as either of
> these two organs desires to exist on its own. The awareness
> of the necessity of that Oneness, once it becomes active, is
> the imagination, which is both love (the highest spiritual
> love) of Nature and the creative principle.

The passage is indeed proof – if proof were needed – of Verwey's profound affinity with Wordsworth. For what he here
wrote discursively as a paraphrase of Wordsworth's Idea of the
Imagination, is matched imaginatively by the final lines of his
own 'Legends', which I quote once more:

> The Ruler comes: his Peace does not bring death,
> But drowns the unrighteousness of twofold life
> In a new mode flawlessly pure and true.
> He our First Origin re-openeth.
> He ousts the phantom of twin natures' strife.[9]
> Creation's act by him is done anew.

That 'the Ruler' who restores man's sense of 'the unity of all'
and thereby brings peace is in fact the Imagination in
Wordsworth's sense, who rules in the hearts of poets when
they are in harmony with Nature, with the Universe, in fact,
is here put beyond doubt. Verwey's affinity with Wordsworth
is not restricted to their views on the nature of the imagination.
In several poems he testified to his love of 'that dear poet, who
could find gladness in the meanest flower'.

There is a passage in a poem of his later years, in which he
likened the growth of a poem in his own mind with that very
spontaneity of Wordsworth described by him elsewhere[10] in
the words:

Wordsworth's poetry is founded on an intimate oneness of poetic composition and thought. Other poets think, and when they presently write a poem, part of their thought [...] passes into what they write. But Wordsworth thought as he wrote, and the thought proved to be a poem.[10]

That he recognised that form of spontaneous poetic thought as his own, is clear from the stanza in question, which I translate as follows – the quotation in Chapter III is repeated here to obviate cross-reference:

How marvellously what's in the heart will grow!
One can dig up a plant with flower and foliage
And root, and, with the dew still on its leaves,
– If handling it with care – transplant it
In other soil; it can be touched by hand,
Its bodily form remains, then as before.
But that a thought should be transplanted from
Our mind, in words communicated,
That is a miracle. He of whom I spoke
Did even more. What he transferred in words
Was far more than a thought, was its arising
Its sprouting, branching out, its consummation
In bud and flower. From a dark tiny seed
It blossomed and still bears its dew of stillness.[11]

Such profound understanding of Wordsworth's mode of poetic thought is rare. It was achieved by Verwey because he found in Wordsworth, his 'thoughtful friend', a sharer of his own 'natural piety' and a fellow-worshipper of that Nature which, to him also, was the 'wisdom and spirit of the universe'.

VI   Verwey and Stefan George:
their conflicting affinities

The relation between two poets who met as contemporaries is naturally far more complex and harder to assess than a poet's relation to a revered master or a kindred predecessor. In the case of these two great personalities it is further complicated by the fact that their encounter soon led to an ambivalent relation. Almost at once they found themselves not only friends, but rivals and exponents of militant spiritual forces that were opposed and were bound to clash sooner or later. The words written by Verwey at George's death still remain the most exact definition of what both united and separated them:

Even death is not strong enough to destroy spiritual bonds of more than personal value. Our alliance was based on corresponding and conflicting tendencies that went much deeper than our personal being, albeit that, with regard to each other, we represented them. They were within us, but they are also of our time, and they will continue to exist in the future.[1]

This ostensibly vague description: 'corresponding and conflicting tendencies', is in fact the only one which includes *all* aspects of their complex relation, for it involved the very foundations of both their personalities.

Their relation has been investigated and described many times already. Some investigators clearly belonged to the circle or sphere of either poet; thus Friedrich Wolters approached Verwey entirely from George's angle, whereas Maurits Uyldert could only view George from Verwey's point of view. But also in other studies of the subject one can discern a more or less one-sided orientation. The one outstanding exception is Rudolf Pannwitz's *Zu Verwey's hundertstem Geburtstag*, in which the essential features of each poet are viewed and formulated with profound insight.

A new detailed study based on the complete records was published in 1968 by Dr Jan Aler, whose *Im Spiegel der Form* has remained one of the indispensable works for the study of George's *Der Stern des Bundes*. Broadly speaking, his conclusion is that, contrary to what was thought hitherto, the 'parting of the ways' must be placed long before the 'Maximin-Erlebniss', and must be attributed to a desire on the part of both poets to over-emphasise their differences for the sake of asserting their independence, or, as Aler puts it: 'Het is dan zaak, de ander vast te leggen op het tegendeel van wat men zelf is, voor zich, en zoals men wenst te blijken in zijn werk.[2] "Dans les domaines de la création, qui sont aussi les domaines de l'orgueil, la nécessité de se distinguer est indivisible de l'existence même."[3] One may agree with this view as regards their relation on the social and public plane, while yet questioning its validity for the two poets' inner lives. Indeed, Aler's study itself, which includes both aspects in its analysis, is there to prove that the relation between their two personalities was complex to a degree. If one takes due note of every hint of difference or of conflicting viewpoints in their correspondence, it is not difficult to demonstrate that, from their very first meeting, both the sense of affinity and the awareness of fundamental differences was present in the two poets' minds. Hence the causes of their final breach are discernible from the first, and so is the fact of their equally fundamental kinship. Once this is realised, the development of their relation is seen to have been a gradual, continuous process, punctuated by a number of realisations of (progressive) estrangement, rather than severed by one decisive turning-point.

As one reads Verwey's account of their first meetings – the only available one – in *Mijn verhouding tot Stefan George*, one senses the initial stages of a mutual approach which took place simultaneously on two levels: a cautious reconnoitring of each other's intellectual, artistic and poetic position, and a spontaneous, mutually generous recognition of an as yet unformulable subconscious affinity. The vicissitudes of their relation will always remain inexplicable unless one sees its growth as the continuous interweaving of these two processes, each variously coloured and modified by the other, into one inextricably tangled pattern: the encounter of two poets of different nationality and background. They felt drawn to each other; their relation swiftly matured into friendship. Yet it was soon shaken by acute conflicts resulting in alienation, and thus ultimately led to a wistfully retrospective affection from afar. Both knew themselves to be pioneers, leaders of their respective movements and exponents of kindred poetic ideas; both realised that the idea of each had its national and universal aspects. But above all they came to realise, after a few years of somewhat over-conscious striving after 'eensgezindheid', that they were at the same time profoundly akin and deeply antagonistic. It is this paradoxical bond of conflicting kinship that renders their relation of such eminent importance in the cultural history of Western Europe.

On the intellectual and political level their encounter led to an irreconcilable conflict between two mutually exclusive attitudes, an autocratic nationalistic and a democratic universalist one, whose development until the crisis of 1910 and the epilogue of 1919 can be traced in the documents. It is a relatively simple process along a fairly straight line. The development of their relation as exponents of their respective poetic ideas is far more intricate and correspondingly more interesting; Aler's study is focused on that process, of which it gives a meticulous and fascinating account. But there was between them a relationship on a yet deeper, almost wholly subconscious level, which by its very nature can only be sensed, divined almost, from their most intimate utterances:

> Het vreemde weten van een dieper bond
> Waarvoor ik in dat uur geen woorden vond.[4]

That is the relationship which remained and went on growing even beyond their final parting – mostly dormant but occasionally showing in some apparently casual utterance. In *Ewiger Augenblick* Robert Boehringer gives an imaginative record of a conversation between George ('Der Meister') and some friends on the subject of his poem 'An die Kinder des Meeres', which Otto called 'ganz unverständlich'. Forder, who apparently knew that the poem contained a hidden reference to Verwey, asked: 'Kam von den einst gastlichen Wogen ein Echo?' Whereupon George thoughtfully said: 'Auf den Abschied schrieb er so:

Die Grenzen die du setzest
Tun dir selbst am meisten weh.
Wenn du dich abscheidest
Du kannst nicht hindern,
Dass wir dir nah sind.'

And, after Rudolf's remark, 'Wie vornehm!' – 'Bewunderungswürdig und christlich. Es macht mich traurig'.[5]

This sign of remaining affection has its counterpart in an undatable utterance of Verwey's, a fragment of a poem (apparently never completed):[6]

Mijn arme koning, ik bemin u zoo
Omdat ge voor een ander mensch u niet
Verneedren kunt en nooit iets af kunt doen
Van d'aangenomen houding, laten u
Allen alleen die niet als ik uw zwakte
Erkennen naast uw grootheid. Niemand weet
Hoezeer ge een kind zijt en hoe hulpeloos
Gevangen in uw eensgekweekte waan
Van onvernederbare majesteit –

Such affection on both sides after their numerous clashes and misunderstandings points to an affinity more fundamental than their antagonism. Its nature can only be guessed at. One aspect of it was conveyed by Verwey in the lines:

Anders gij dan ik.
Al de inhouden van uw wezen
Anders dan de mijne elk ogenblik.
Anders gij dan ik.
[...]
Waar is 't wonder dan
Dat twee levenslang gescheidnen
Nochtans levenslang verenen kan.
Waar is 't wonder dan?

Iedre zin is vreemd.
't Zij zo: in ons beider denken
Niets dat naar 't gedenk van de andre zweemt.
Iedre zin is vreemd.

Maar zijn vorm bekoort.
Iedre toonval vast verstaanbaar,
Iedre lijn en schakeling en woord.
Zie, zijn vorm bekoort.
[...]
Vorm aan vorm verwant
Heffen zich twee vreemdling-zielen
Aan de kimmen elk van 't eigen land –
Vorm aan vorm verwant.

Noem het liefde of haat:
Siddrend groeten bei elkander,
Daar hun open oog elks vorm verstaat.
Noem het liefde of haat.[7]

The awareness of kinship is here seen to be a mutual recognition of kindred form – and this must be taken to include the inner form which shows in the very structure of the personality, the 'shape of the soul' – witness the lines

Meer dan zin en geest,
Als aan de uiting voor-geboren,
Leeft in ons de Vorm, de ziele-leest,
Meer dan zin en geest.[8]

It includes even the form of their thought – though not its content. After all, both poets were convinced of the oneness of soul and body; both were aware that in (George) or through (Verwey) a human countenance one could see the divine. George once wrote:

Als ich am andren abend bei dir sass
Merkt ich wie durch dein erstes durch: das zweite
Das gottesantlitz langsam dir erwächst.[9]

This is closely paralleled in the opening lines of Verwey's poem 'Mijn Meester':

Staat gij niet achter menslijke aangezichten,
Mijn lieve meester, als een nieuw gelaat
Dat heenschijnt door het oude? En zijn de trekken

Waar droomgelijk we uw wezen door ontdekken
Ons hart niet dierbaar als de dageraad
Voor wie begeren dat de zon zal lichten?[10]

Yet there is a fundamental difference, which becomes unmistakable in George's 'gottesantlitz'. With Verwey, a revelation of divine reality may be seen as a passing illumination in any human face; with George one human countenance becomes divine:

Dem bist du kind, dem freund.
Ich seh in dir den Gott
Den schauernd ich erkannt
Dem meine andacht gilt.[11]

If one confronts this confession of faith with Verwey's considered – and considerate – response in 'Emmäusganger':

In de gestalte zien wat andren dromen,
Wat voor de meesten vaag verlangen blijft,
Dat was uw voorrecht, Vriend. Een nevel drijft
Dan voor uw oog en 't beeld is weggenomen....[12]

one is driven to the conclusion that the realisation of incompatibility in the innermost personal and poetic sphere can, nay, must be placed in the two poets' irreconcilable interpretations of George's Maximim-Erlebniss. Yet the interpretation of neither was rigid; each had his moments of uncertainty. Thus, in the 'Teuflische Stanze',[13] written before George met Maximilian Kronberger and published anonymously in the *Blätter für die Kunst,* which was credibly attributed to George, the telling opening line startlingly reveals a deep scepticism of the genuineness of such an experience: 'Noch jeder Gott war menschliches geschöpfe...,' And long after Maximilian's death George wondered:

War der gott der mir erleuchtet
War der geist der mir erschienen
Fern aus unermessnen höhn?
Hab ich selber ihn geboren?
Schweig gedanke! seele bete![14]

If he, then, knew his moments of doubt, Verwey has his times of bearing and almost sympathising with George's poetic theogony:

> ... Ik kende een vriend die smeekte
> Dat hem een god verscheen. Zijn denken kweekte
> De god, zijn wezen, zijn verschijning, tot
> Hij ze uitschreef, en daarná verscheen de god.
> Een werklijkheid, maar door hemzelf geschapen,
> Of slechts gezien? In alle dingen slapen
> Mogelijkheden, talloos, en ons oog
> Legt in de wereld wat ons hart bewoog.
> Ik ook smeekte om een god, om een volledig
> Leven, rond afgesloten, evenredig
> In al zijn delen, ganslijk buiten mij.
> ...
> Mijn god kwam anders dan ik dacht. Diep uit
> Mijn heerlijkst leven trad hij aan, volkomen
> En stralend, en heeft mij 't gezicht benomen
> Op al het andre...[15]

A sympathetic recognition of George's experience, but not an acceptance of his faith. The drama of this friendship is nowhere more moving than in such passages. We see how profound was their imaginative and emotional affinity, we realise how the inevitable and irrevocable parting of their ways must have wounded both in the tenderest fibres of their souls. Whereas, at any confrontation, each would have rejected the other's point of view, each in his heart would sometimes wonder whether there was not, somewhere hidden within him, a doubt, a leaning towards the other's position, through which he could almost approach him, or at any rate imaginatively identify himself with him for a moment. It should not be forgotten that each poet believed in the possibility of a divine revelation to him personally, and in human form. That it was so for George is well known, but a number of poems by Verwey record imaginative experiences of a numinous nature, in which the divine countenance assumed a visible and almost tangible form.[16]

Where then lies the essential difference? Not in the entire

absence, in Verwey's case, of such revelations in actual encounters; for although, to my knowledge, there is no record, poetic or otherwise, of such an experience, Verwey could hardly have written that the Master's countenance 'stands, as a new-born face, behind human countenances', if such experiences had never been his. The difference is not one of experience, but of interpretation. As George studied the revered friend's face, he witnessed the divine countenance slowly maturing there; as Verwey saw a human face irradiated with unearthly light, he was aware of the divine countenance behind it. It should be remembered that George, who grew up as the son of devout Catholic parents, in his youth had self-evidently received the Eucharist as a sacrament, whereas Verwey, brought up in the Protestant tradition, naturally saw the Last Supper as a religious symbol. I believe that ultimately the difference between them lies in their respective interpretations of numinous experiences, Verwey's thought being symbolic and mystical, George's sacramental.

In poets, a fundamental difference such as this is bound to originate in an equally fundamental difference between their modes of poetic thought. Such a difference can indeed be shown to exist. George's thought in 'Das Wort' is characteristic and unmistakable:

Wunder von ferne oder traum
Bracht ich an meines landes saum

Und harrte bis die graue norn
Den namen fand in ihrem born—

Drauf konnt ichs greifen dicht und stark—[17]

But once she failed to reveal the name of a priceless gem the poet had found:

Sie suchte lang und gab mir kund:
'So schläft hier nichts auf tiefem grund',

Worauf es meiner hand entrann
Und nie mein land den schatz gewann...

So lernt ich traurig den verzicht:
Kein ding sei wo das wort gebricht.

This is sacramental thought. If the embodiment of a sacred conception is not realised, the truth cannot be apprehended and is lost.

The poem was published as part of *Das Neue Reich,* of which Verwey in 1928 received a copy 'übersandt vom verfasser'. His own volume *Het Lachende Raadsel* (The Smiling Enigma) (1935), of which the middle section entitled 'Bij de dood van een vriend' (On the death of a friend) is entirely concerned with the memory of George, in its first, chronologically earlier section contains the poem 'Het verborgen vuur' (The Hidden Fire), of which the subject is closely related to that of 'Das Wort'. It would not be fantastic to suppose that it might conceivably constitute a cryptic answer to it; the curious echo of George's rhyme kund: grund in Verwey's rhyme kond: grond, an almost archaic rhyme rare in twentieth-century poetry and indeed in Verwey's own verse, may well be more than a coincidence.

Toen was ik jong, nu ben ik oud.
Wat is het onderscheid gering.
De maand valt in hetzelfd seizoen,
Het middaguur is nog als toen,
En ik zit hier, die saamspraak houd
Met hen en met mijn mijmering.

The nature of his thought has not changed. And, he observes,

En mijn gedachten zijn vandaag
Nog even vast, nog even vaag:
Gewaringen door taal getucht,
Maar elke een onbegrepen vond.[18]

His intuitive perceptions are indeed disciplined, controlled by language; but they are not dependent on it, they lead their own life:

Hoe vreemd dat de gedachten gaan
En spreken zich volkomen uit
En dat hun zin, hoe openbaar,
Toch anders is, en even klaar
Op een ook thans weer onverstaan,
Een nooit ontraadseld weten duidt.

Will the mystery one day unfold and be revealed in its entirety?
he wonders. The illusion is dear and dies hard:

Maar 't kan niet zijn. Op 't effen doek
Van uw verbeelding teken ik
De schaduw die dit brandend vuur
Werpt door mijn zichtbare natuur,
Ik dwaas die vuur in schaduw zoek
En eeuwig in een ogenblik.

De beelden die mijn eeuwig licht
Op tijdlijk wisselen verwon,
Die laat ik u en 't is genoeg.
Ik weet dat ik geen schaduw joeg,
Maar ook dat tot geen oog de zon
Zijn onverhulde stralen richt.[19]

The contrast is clear-cut and profoundly illuminating. It reveals a radically different view of the relation between conception and creation in poetry. George seeks the word, the form which shall perpetuate the 'wunder' by embodying it in a consummate creation, a 'ding'. Verwey thoughtfully utters words which cast shadow-images of the incommunicable reality on the reader's mind. These images are strangely elusive and always leave something yet more profound unsaid. They are, after all, shadows, and the poet is, wisely though not sadly, aware of his folly in 'seeking fire in shadow'. But reality can wait. If one image proves weak or faulty, he trusts that others will come along to fulfil its function. The invisible, uncommunicable reality remains, irrespective of the poet's utterance. George's revelation is 'einmalig', it can only be embodied in the one unrepeatable, once-for-all-given experience that must be recorded integrally, or it is lost for ever. Hence 'He sadly learned to be resigned', whereas Verwey's acceptance of the poet's limited power was voiced in the trusting lines:

> I know mine was no shadow-chase,
> But on no living eye the sun
> Will ever cast his unveiled rays.

We have now come as near as possible to the foundations of the two poets' creative impulses–and have once more met the unbridgeable chasm that separates them. But this was to be expected.

Long before these two poems came into being, Verwey wrote the lines quoted above culminating in the line: 'Vorm aan vorm verwant...' Now, as we concentrate our attention on the all-embracing form which determines the overall structure of entire works, we are faced with the contrast already observed on p.43: George is a poetic architect who arranges his poems, irrespective of their date of origin, as so many stones to form a grandiose building; Verwey sees them growing gradually, one by one, and in the end *discovers* that, unintentionally and at first unknown to himself, they form a living *organism*.[20]

Verwey naturally observed this: in his own poetry he saw the images emerging from a stream, in George's the images encased in a harmonious frame: '*Der Teppich des Lebens*' '*Der Siebente Ring*'. Yet, again as Pannwitz observed, we do sometimes find Verwey's poems in a firm framework, as in *Godenschemering* and in *De Legenden van de Ene Weg*, and George's in a stream of lyrics, e.g. in the lyrical cycles *Die Lieder von Traum und Tod* and *Das Lied*. It is here, in the flowing form, that the affinity of the two poets can be observed. In Verwey's volume *Het Zichtbaar Geheim* (The Visible Mystery) there is a poem which is in fact a portrait of the Dutch pre-romantic poet Rhynvis Feith (1753–1824), as Verwey imagined seeing him at his country-seat Boschwijk; his name is not mentioned:

Vizioen op Boschwijk

Binnen de donkre cirkelmuur,
Met riet gedekt,
Van voren open naar het uitzicht toe
Van weiden onder 't zwaar gebladert door
Van weerzijds linde en eik,
Zit hij en leest.
Erachter is de kom,
De zwarte vijver,
Waarrondom linden staan.
De grijze dag is over 't weiland zilver,
De leeuwrik rijst, de koeien grazen,
De verre horizon leeft roerloos-rijk,–
Hij leest en schrijft.
De blaadren achter hem zijn vol gesuis,
Het water vloeit onhoorbaar saam,
De donkre schaduwen zijn vormloos stil,–
Hij zit in schaduw en hij schrijft en peinst.
En stilte en verte en scheemring en geluid
Vloeien ineen tot woorden…
Hij peinst en schreit.[21]

Everything is evoked, both as to sight and sound, but subdued
and enveloped in an atmosphere of thoughtful melancholy –
Feith's poetic atmosphere, in fact. The means by which this is
achieved are not easy to ascertain at first sight. A similar effect
can be observed in George's 'Lied':

Fern von des hafens lärm
Ruht der besonnte strand,
Zittern die wellen aus..
Hoffnung vergleitet sacht.

Da regt vom hohen meer
Wind die gewölbten auf,
Bäumend zerkrachen sie,
Stürmend die ufer ein..
Wie nun das leiden tost!

Lautere brandung rauscht,
Zischend zur dünenhöh
Schlägt sie den dunklen schaum..
Wie nun die liebe stöhnt![22]

Both poems are evocative, and in each the scene evoked sym-
bolises feelings, though in George's case they *develop* as the
scene changes, whereas the mood in Verwey's poem is static
like the landscape. The kindred poetic techniques that produce
these effects were, in point of fact, characterised by Verwey in
two lines of a poem addressed to George:[23]

Wij hebben bei den adem die het woord
Boetseert zodat uit klank gestalte wordt.

This evocative 'modelling' is achieved, not by description
alone, but by the varying length of the lines which is the out-
come of the natural breathing of the poet who *imagines* himself
speaking the lines. In 'Vizioen op Boschwijk', the breath
groups[24] represented by the individual lines are such that each
line constitutes a glance of the eye or an impression on the ear
that adds a touch to the total picture.

In George's poem the feelings change with the sea. Further-
more, each poem also contains somewhat longer breathing
pauses, by which it falls into a kind of (rhymeless) stanzas
which are rhythmic although not of equal length; and the closing line of each 'stanza' is an explicit utterance of the feeling
suggested indirectly in the preceding lines; in Verwey's poem
these are:

–Zit hij en leest
–Hij leest en schrijft.
–Hij zit in schaduw en hij schrijft en peinst.
–Hij peinst en schreit.

The rhymeless poem thus consists of such 'stanzas' respectively of 6, 7, 4 and 3 lines. In George's case also the feeling is
expressed directly in the lines

–Hoffnung vergleitet sacht
–Wie nun das leiden tost!
–Wie nun die liebe stöhnt!

His 'stanzas', also rhymeless, likewise differ in length; they are
of 4, 5 and 4 lines respectively. Such unintentional, wholly
spontaneous correspondence in structure is the unmistakable
sign of that profound affinity which each poet intuitively recognised in the other – a recognition that caused Verwey to
write:

> Noem het liefde of haat;
> Siddrend groeten bei elkander
> Daar hun open oog elks vorm verstaat.[25]

There remains the mystery of the affinity felt by both poets,
which neither of them really managed to define. Perhaps it will
always escape rational analysis. But they did sometimes *convey*
it in a poem. One of George's most radiant visions of felicity
was evoked in the following lines:

> Von welchen wundern lacht die morgen-erde
> Als wär ihr erster tag? Erstauntes singen
> Von neu-erwachten welten trägt der wind
> Verändert sieht der alten berge form
> Und wie im kindheit-garten schaukeln blüten...
> Der strom besprengt die ufer und es schlang
> Sein zitternd silber allen staub der jahre
> Die schöpfung schauert wie im stand der gnade.
> Kein gänger kommt des weges dessen haupt
> Nicht eine ungewusste hoheit schmücke.
> Ein breites licht ist übers land gegossen...
> Heil allen die in seinen strahlen gehn![26]

Although ostensibly this is a vision of the pristine glory of the
youthful earth, its true character as a foreshadowing of *future*
felicity is conveyed by the poem immediately following it:

> Dies ist reich des Geistes: abglanz
> Meines reiches, hof und hain.
> Neugestaltet umgeboren
> Wird hier jeder: ort der wiege,
> Heimat bleibt ein märchenklang.

A remarkable parallel is the following sonnet written by Verwey in 1903:

Ziet ge niet, o mijn ziel? –De bomen blozen,
Velden zijn bloemenvol onder de zon,
Beken springen te voorschijn of een spon
Uit een vol vat sloeg: dauwig staan de rozen,

Waartussen zangvogels zingen en kozen
–o Wie als zij zingen en kozen kon–
En alsof eeuwge morgenstond begon
Stijgt van gediert geluid en zwijgt bij pozen.

Zie wie daar komen! Mensen, opgericht
In schoner stand dan we op onze aard ooit zagen.
Hoe groot en vrij hun blik: zijn handen dragen

Een vrucht, zij leidt een lam; maar wilde dieren
Volgen hen stil door die schone revieren,
Lettend gehoorzaam op hun hoog gezicht.[27]

The vision is so strongly reminiscent of Vondel's paradise tragedy *Adam in Ballingschap* (First Act) that the effect is one of a reborn Adam and Eve as bearers of a future, happier state of mankind.

Both poets were seers with a firm faith in a better, more beautiful humanity that was to come one day. In moments of vision both saw in the sunlit present the foreshadowing of that future, in the light of imagination which is the light of the spirit:

Sieh, dieser Sonnentag sprengt jede grenze
Die zeiten vor und nach begreift er ein.[28]

In his 'Conversations with one who died' (the painter Floris Verster) Verwey wrote:

Only a few are bearers of the light,
The light that's in the spirit and whose rays

Break in the world and find their image there
In light of nature as it breaks on earth.[29]

and he recognised in George a seeker and a lover of that light:

By the radiance of the lofty lamp
He knew the light he loved and fearlessly
He cast himself before thee, he alighted and
With unrestrained, courageous winged passion
Encircled thy quiet rays....[30]

That George knew himself to be a bearer of the light of the
spirit, was once more movingly expressed in one of his last
songs:

Wir sind in trauer wenn, uns minder günstig
Du dich zu andren, mehr beglückten, drehst
Wenn unser geist, nach anbetungen brünstig,
An abenden in deinem abglanz wes't.

Wir wären töricht, wollten wir dich hassen
Wenn oft dein strahl verderbendrohend sticht
Wir wären kinder, wollten wir dich fassen—
Da du für alle leuchtest, süsses Licht![31]

It was after George's death in 1933 that Verwey in his 'Songs of
Ultimate Understanding' once more meditated on their relation and its unsolved mystery, still experiencing the conflicting
affinity that had thrilled and tormented each of them, until he
found

The enduring union of your song and mine,
The wave to which your body lends its line.[32]

and saw that the fundamental element they shared was their
form, that the dream they had in common was the light which
is revealed only in song. The miracle that delivered him from
the sense of conflict was: Song at peace within itself; the
radiant light of timeless singing.

VII The Universe, a vision of man

Verwey's transformation of a landscape description by Southey

In *Rondom mijn Werk,* Verwey's own anthology of occasional poems not published in book form, there is a poem entitled 'Southey voor Derwentwater', a vivid evocation of a windless moment on the well-known lake in Cumberland, so graphic and ostensibly spontaneous that the title seems strange.[1] Was the scene imagined by Verwey–as is quite possible, since he of course knew that most of Southey's life was spent at Greta Hall near Keswick–and did he, quite naturally, picture Southey here as gazing on Derwentwater? But why did he place the poem between quotation marks, thus representing it as actually spoken by Southey? One can't help wondering whether it is a translation of one of his poems. But no such poem is to be found in Southey's published work. There are, indeed, poems in which Derwentwater is mentioned or even described, but none of these descriptions bears any resemblance to Verwey's poem. There is one remarkable fact, however: the poem is dated 12.7.1912, and 1912 is the very year in which a collection of Southey's letters appeared: *Letters of Robert Southey – a Selection.* This surely is more than a coincidence. In point of fact the selection contains the following letter, which is addressed to George Grosvenor Bedford, a friend of the poet. Its first half – the sequel is of no interest here – is as follows:

> Dear Grosvenor, I have seen a sight more dreamy and wonderful than any scenery that fancy ever yet devised for faery-land. We had walked down to the lakeside; it was a delightful day, the sun shining, and a few white clouds hanging motionless in the sky. The opposite shore of Derwentwater consists of one long mountain, which suddenly terminates in an arch, thus ⌣, and through that opening you see a long valley between mountains, and bounded by mountain

beyond mountain; to the right of the arch the heights are more varied and of greater elevation. Now, as there was not a breath of air stirring, the surface of the lake was so perfectly still, that it became one great mirror, and all the waters disappeared; the whole line of shore was represented as vividly and steadily as it existed in its actual being – the arch, the vale within, the single houses far within the vale, the smoke from their chimneys, the farthest hills, and the shadow and substance joined at their bases so indivisibly, that you could make no separation even in your judgement. As I stood on the shore, heaven and the clouds seemed lying under me; I was looking down into the sky, and the whole range of mountains, having one line of summits under my feet, and another above me, seemed to be suspended between the firmaments. Shut your eyes and dream of a scene so unnatural and so beautiful. What I have told is most strictly and scrupulously true; but it was one of those happy moments that can seldom occur, for the least breath stirring would have shaken the whole vision, and at once unrealized it. I have before seen a partial appearance, but never before did, and perhaps never again may, lose sight of the lake entirely; for it literally seemed like an abyss of sky before me, not fog and clouds from a mountain, but the blue heaven spotted with a few fleecy pillows of cloud, that looked placed there for angels to rest upon them.

This wonderful description was doubtless Verwey's source, as my (very close) rendering will show:[2]

Southey regarding Derwentwater

One moment's span: the mere was still,
So still, it seemed a mere no more,
 No water and no wind did stir,
But mirror-power alone was there,

A double landscape, down, above,
Where clear and tenuous each thing stood,
Motionless even what did move:
The chimney-smoke that yonder showed.

There was a mountain-ridge whose line
Abruptly sank, then to ascend,
And, plainly seen, a long ravine –
And meadow, trees and cottage gained

A brightness, an uncommon light
From mid-day's hour; reflection was
So wholly an unbroken sight
With the reality – the glass

Of water was not recognised,
But double heaven, double earth
From foreground to the farthest rise,
Uncleavable yet twofold both,

Seemed hanging in a wondrous sphere,
A world under so strange a spell,
That as I gazed I knew no more
If all was dream, or dream the All.

One moment's pause: a waft of air,
A rippling makes the still shapes flow:
I see the mere, I see the shore;
The Deep divides: on high – below.

Verwey followed Southey's description of the landscape even
to the smallest details, and in the identical order. But his opening and closing lines are different. The short duration of this
windless moment is not mentioned in the opening passage of
Southey's letter; it is only after his words: 'Shut your eyes and
dream of a scene so unnatural and so beautiful' that he
observes: 'It was one of those happy moments that can seldom
occur, for the least breath stirring would have shaken the
whole vision' – without stating that this was what did in fact
happen. He mentions it as a possible event; it is not an essential
element of his experience.

In Verwey's poem that momentary character of the experience, which became his own, is its very essence: 'Eén ogenblik'
and 'Eén oogwenk maar' open and close the evocation, thus
determining the cyclical form of this sequence of 7 quatrains.

In the poem everything is simultaneous, inseparable. Unlike Southey, who first described the actual landscape, and only then related how the motionless lake reflected it all 'as vividly and steadily as it existed in its actual being', Verwey transforms Southey's description into the evocation of a *single* phenomenon. Southey's amazed utterance: 'the shadow and substance joined at their bases so indivisibly that you could make no separation' which *follows* his description, forms Verwey's initial statement of this inseparable oneness of the landscape and its reflected image: 'een dubbellandschap, laag en hoog.' With both poets the experience is felt to be a miracle. But their sense of wonder over this miracle is not of the same kind. Southey saw it as 'truth stranger than fiction', or, in his own words 'a sight more dreamy and wonderful than any scenery that fancy ever yet devised for faeryland' – in fact, as a fantasmal image too beautiful for this world.

Verwey absorbs Southey's landscape picture and, in transforming it into his strophically formed poem, becomes aware that it was

> a landscape in a strange universe,
> at which I gazed and knew no more
> if the cosmos was a dream or (my) dream the cosmos.

Before his enigmatic line 'was 't Al een droom of droom het Al', each half of which is a mirror-image of the other, the reader pauses and ponders. One senses the presence of a profound symbol, the significance of which slowly detaches itself from our confused thoughts. The symbol is both contained and concealed in the double image of the landscape. The former alternative 'Was 't Al een droom' is in harmony with Southey's utterance, '... and dream of a scene so unnatural and so beautiful', but the latter alternative contained in the second half-line goes beyond it, seeing that the poet here wonders if the universe could be the creation of a 'dream', and that is to say that for Verwey the universe only *exists* because Man creates it in his 'dream' – his imagination – and only thus *sees* it, not as manifold, but as one.

This concept, the core of Verwey's view of life, is, in this poem, both expressed and concealed in a symbolic image.

Such more or less concealed symbols of Verwey's vision of the universe are to be found in a number of his poems. It was in one late poem of 1934, 'De Bekoring' ('The Enchantment') that he expressed it openly:

> Lo, Man's the creature beautiful, the Prince of Earth,
> The one whose mind receives all things.
> He shaped each thing, and he revealed
> In song and word the almost inexpressible.
> What is his Dream? the Universe, – 'twas made by him.[3]

It is only a clear insight into Verwey's variously expressed (and concealed!) images of this concept that will bring out the profundity of this transformation of Southey's landscape portrayal. Southey saw the double landscape as a dream-image from faeryland; Verwey as a momentary perception of the Vision that is identical with the Universe itself. Hence his sad realisation in the final quatrain: 'één oogwenk maar' – for one instant only did he experience the *visible* oneness of the truly imagined Universe. Once the motionless reflection of the landscape was disturbed and destroyed, reality returned to its divided form that is part of daily experience: the unity of landscape and mirroring water was split into two abysses, once more separated: the apparently empty heaven on high, and the no-longer-mirroring lake down below – symbolic of the normal experience even for the poet: *here* the lack-lustre world of everyday life, *there* the dimmed dream, that is no longer beheld in its splendour.

Was Verwey justified in ascribing *this* experience to Southey, as his quotation marks suggest? The problem can hardly be resolved. Southey wrote a letter to a friend, and his experience did not – as far as we know – mature into a poem. But he must have felt more than he was able to express – he did, after all, refer to the 'abyss of sky' down below. He knew the sense of infinity on beholding a beautiful landscape. In his poem 'A Vision of Judgment', a description of Derwentwater shortly before sunset ends with the impressive lament: 'And as I gazed in the West, where Infinity seemed to be open, Yearned to be free from time, and felt that this life is a thraldom.'

The conviction that the universe is a vision, a 'dream' of the human imagination, can be shown to be an essential aspect of Verwey's view of life. Perhaps the most perfect symbol of this among his short lyrics is 'Praying Youth', the closing poem of his last completed volume 'The Fever of the Ephemeral'. The poet addresses a young man who is portrayed as the mythical bearer of the dream. His statuesque form embodies one desire: to embrace the universe with the imagination. In silent adoration, tense like a bow held by an unseen hand, he prays, wordless, neither asking nor lamenting, while he raises a bowl bearing invisible flames – the fire of his yearning. His silent prayer finds its answer in that very tension: he proves to be the motionless axis round which the universe, visible only to man's imagination, revolves. He *is* the embodied vision of the universe.

One mystery still remains. The youth is 'A lovely bow that's tautly drawn, Held by a likewise unseen hand'. By what hand? one inevitably wonders. These two lines are of vital significance, for a bow serves the hand of an archer. Who is he? The mystery can be elucidated by referring to an earlier poem, 'De Bevrijding' ('Liberation'),[4] of 1918. The following passage has a bearing on our problem; I translate:

Love alone is fearless and courageous,
Alone is wholly free, –
...
Like a line, a beam
One single arrow streams forth from the soul
Of the universe through all souls, and the world
Knows that it must revolve round that one arrow.

Love, eternal love, is the soul of the universe, and is the origin of everything:

Instinct that is love! with what other name
Canst thou be named, steel arrow! Thou wert shot
Forth by the godlike Archer. Standing upright
On the watchtower of the universe, he saw
His aim, far beyond ages, raised his bow
And shot the arrow through infinite space.

In this poem, written eighteen years before 'Praying Youth', the metaphor, though not identical, shows considerable affinity, sufficient to elucidate the later poem. The youth is the embodied yearning of Man to be one with the universe, and his yearning is the instrument that serves the universal soul. That soul, the 'godlike Archer', holds him and guides him. The wordless yearning of this youth is inspired by Divine Love itself. The poem is the crowning image of Verwey's monumental work – the statuesque symbol of the core of his faith in mankind.

Part II

Poems with translations

Foreword

Translating poems is a precarious venture. One aims at an ideal which by its very nature is unattainable; for it goes without saying that no translation can ever match the original. The poet P.N. van Eyck was aware of this when he called his verse translations 'Approximations'.

Indeed. No translator can do more than approximate. But it *is* possible for him to give readers who do not know the poet's language or have only a smattering of it, some impression of the poem.

Now there are connoisseurs of poetry who claim that one can only render a poem adequately *in prose*. In their opinion a translation which aims at retaining the prosodic form falls short of the original to a greater extent than a prose translation. Others, however, hold the view that the form of the original is essential and indispensable.

From the translations printed here it can be inferred that I belong to the latter group. Why? – the reader will ask. Does not the retention of the rhythmical or even the metrical form compel the translator to render the 'content' more freely, sometimes even inaccurately?

No one will deny that this is so. – But – we are not only concerned with the paraphrasable content of the poem. A poem worthy of the name must come to life afresh in the reader's imagination. How can this be brought about? By enabling him to *hear* the poem and to visualize it. It is very hard to determine *how* this is brought about. Actually the reader of poetry knows this by experience only. If he tries to analyse that experience, he becomes aware that, far more than the words in their context – i.e. the paraphrasable content of the poem – it is the sound pattern, the rhythm and the imagery in the widest sense that produce this effect on the reader. These are the creative elements in all poetry. As soon as a poem is stripped of them, it ceases to be a poem – the poetic element has gone.

Perhaps an incident from my experience may be helpful here. Years ago I wished to gain an impression of Troubadour poetry. So I bought or borrowed a number of French editions of their works. Most of these give prose renderings of the Provençal text, which is translated as literally as possible. Now, what impression did I gain from these translations which, with my minimal knowledge of Provençal, I absolutely needed? None whatever. The poems remained wholly obscure to me, as poetry. Not until, in desperation, I set to work with a dictionary and, having more or less ascertained the sense of the individual words, I read the Provençal lines aloud – my pronunciation must have been odd indeed! – did the poetry of the Troubadours come to life for me.

In order to simplify matters, let us assume for the moment that my view is reasonable, so that, in consequence, the translator should try to retain the form of the poem. Does it follow, then, that he should copy the rhythm, the metre, the rhyme scheme, the stanza form, *exactly*? No, he need not do so. The translator does what he can; he does not attempt to do what is beyond his power; after all, his work has an ancillary function. He *approximates*. He restricts himself to what is possible for him personally.

What does this mean in practice? This question is so limitless that I must confine myself to a few briefly formulated remarks.

1   *Rhythm* is the most essential requirement. By this I mean not merely the cadence of the lines (which can be scanned), but also the harmony or deliberate disharmony of the vowels and consonants, the pauses, the run-on lines, the surging and ebbing-away of the volume of sound. These are the features which the translator must try to render first of all. If he sees his way to retain the metre as well – fine; but the rhythm must not be sacrificed to it.

2   *Rhyme*   This is out of fashion at present; but in course of time that is likely to change. But it is a fact that striving to achieve rhyme, especially 'pure' rhyme, can be a danger to the poet. Even more so for the translator. Verlaine, though a magician of rhyme as no other, wrote, in his *Art poétique*: 'Oh, qui dira les torts de la Rime!' In my view, the translator should use

only those rhymes which, so to speak, offer themselves to him. If he 'becomes inspired', they will sometimes actually come spontaneously, almost as if at that moment a poet had taken possession of him; what happens to him then is faintly like that which Verwey once described as follows:

> Did not
> The melody within me – soundless play, –
> Surge into firm and ringing sounds; did not
> My words, as 't were so many brides-elect
> Before their King, range themselves readily
> And gladly? and whoever by the unseen ray
> Of song was struck, would thrill and shiver, bow,
> And come like rushing into opened arms.

Indeed, the translator is merely a modest servant; but something of that spirit must take possession of him, or else his work will remain tinkering. Hence he will make use of those rhymes only that come of their own accord. But he will never twist the train of thought or the metaphoric structure for the sake of a rhyme. Yet this need not lead to complete absence of rhyme. Sometimes consonant rhyme or assonance may enable him to achieve a similar, though weaker effect.

3   Metaphor   This must be retained as faithfully as possible. In case of necessity the translator will sacrifice to it rhyme or metre or even normal syntactical structure – since metaphor in the widest sense is the most visually evocative element.

4   The semantic aspect   Naturally any translator will follow the train of thought of the original as closely as possible. But in my opinion he is justified in reserving more freedom in this respect than as regards rendering rhythm and metaphor. It stands to reason that he will in most cases follow the text. But this must not lead to undue levelling of the rhythm or twisting of the evocative elements of the poem. Such levelling or twisting should be avoided, if need be, by translating more freely. Here we find ourselves in conflict with the view mentioned above, that the semantic element, the paraphrasable 'content' of the poem, is claimed to be of the first importance. Whoever thinks exegetically only, will never be prepared to accept a rendering in verse. Nevertheless even he cannot escape the necessity that *any* translation of a poem, even the most exact rendering in prose, is a personal interpretation. *His* translation, however, is mainly or even exclusively an interpretation of the semantic aspect of the text, not of its imaginative aspect. Hence he ignores the irrefutable fact that a poem is in the first place an imaginative utterance, which can only fully be realised by the imagination of the reader. The translator's first care should be to preserve as much as possible of the impact made by the poem on the imagination. In a prose translation there are not sufficient means to do this – unless the translator gives a strongly rhythmical rendering – and, in doing so, draws nearer to verse again.

It is only by giving his first attention to form that the translator can, to a modest degree, activate the imagination and induce a poetic experience. *Mutatis mutandis*, even he should observe Goethe's maxim: 'Bilde, Künstler – rede nicht.'

Anangke

Toen zag ik aan een meer, het meer des doods,
Een vrouw met vaal gelaat en geluw haar;
Zij schepte 't water op, maar liet altoos
De droppels vallen, alle na elkaar.

En daar ik bij haar stond zo vraagde ik haar; –
Maar zij zag op noch om, bewegingloos:
'Ik heb een vriend: is haast de droppel daar,
Waar hij mee valt, of gunt ge'm nog een poos?'

En wijl de droppels vielen, sprak zij zacht:
'Ziet gij die golf, die zich hierheen beweegt?
Straks zult gij zien wanneer zij naderkomt,
Hoe al haar ruisen aan mijn voet verstomt; –
Als dan mijn hand zich op en neer beweegt
Valt ook zijn leven klankloos in den nacht'.

Een Zomeravond

De poëzie komt over me als een droom
Van sterren en een liefelijke nacht
Van duister, waar me een hel gelaat uit licht
En vriendlijke ogen – enkel dat gelaat,
Want al de rest is nevel zonder vorm.
En heel den nacht nijg ik me er heen en houd
Stille gemeenschap tot de morgen daagt. –
Dan lig ik stil met half geloken wimpers
Te staren waar ik telkens nog den lach
Dier ogen meen te zien en 't blonde haar
Half over 't voorhoofd – dan zijgt zijwaarts af
Mijn hoofd in 't kussen en ik slaap in 't licht.

Anangke

Then by a lake, the lake of death, I saw
A woman sallow-faced with yellow hair;
She scooped up water, but then evermore
Let the drops fall in turn, all those there were.

And standing by her side I questioned her; –
But she looked neither up nor round, quite still:
'I have a friend: will soon the drop be there
With which he'll fall, or grant'st thou him a while?'

And as the drops still fell, she softly said:
'Seest thou that wave there, which is hither bound?
Thou soon shalt see, when nearer it has come,
How all its murmur at my foot grows dumb; –
When I shall then move up and down my hand,
His life, too, shall fall soundless into night.'

A summer evening

A poem has come over me – a dream
Where many stars shine in a tender night
Of darkness, and I see a radiant face
And friendly eyes – only that face I see
Because all else is veiled in formless mist.
And all night long I'm drawn to it and hold
Quiet communion till the morning dawns. –
Then I lie still with eyelashes half closed,
Gazing to where I now and then still seem
To see those smiling eyes and the blond hair
Wavelike over the brow – then on my pillow
I slip head sideways, sleeping in the light.

Het verlaten huis

Als in een huis in de onderwereld, waar
De stille vader en het stomme kind
Elkander aanzien – zó zit ik gebukt
Over mijn boeken in dit donkre huis.
En tegenover me aan de tafel zit
Dat stomme kind der sombere gedachte,
Mijn stille weemoed met het bleek gelaat,
Mijn stomme weemoed met het donker oog,
Die niemand ziet dan ik, – maar als ik opzie,
Dan voel ik dat zij mij heeft aangezien,
Maar 't niet wil weten om die grote smart; –
En als verschrikt buig ik dan weer het hoofd
Achter mijn boeken en ik durf niet spreken
Tot haar, schoon ik gedenk aan vroegre vreugd.
En als gevoelloos, werk ik al den dag
En zie niet op noch om, omdat ik vrees
De grote smart, die 'k zien zal in dat oog.
Want zij was eens zo schoon, mijn jonge weemoed,
Toen alle bloemen blij ons tegenbloeiden
En vogels spotten met ons jeugdig leed.
Maar weggedoken zit de laatste vogel
Thans in de takken en door de enge spleet
Der half gesloten blinden valt het licht
Op ons, die treuren in 't verlaten huis. –

Van de liefde die vriendschap heet

Licht mijner ziel! ik zag u steeds van ver,
En wist wel dat gij eindlijk komen zoudt; –
Woorden, die ik nog niemand heb betrouwd,
Gaan uit als bleke vlammen; – als een ster,

Diep in 't azuur, maar blanker, lieflijker,
Zie 'k in uw lokken liggen 't licht gelaat;
't Mysterie van veel leeds, maar nooit van haat,
Droomt in uw ogen; – 'k zag het steeds van ver.

The deserted house

As in a house in nether regions, where
The quiet father and the speechless child
Regard each other – so do I sit bowed
Over my books in this dark house.
And facing me is sitting at the table
That speechless child of sombre thought,
My quiet wistfulness with her pale face,
My speechless wistfulness with her dark eye,
Whom no one sees but I, – but, looking up,
I feel that she has just regarded me,
But tries to hide it, as her grief is great; –
And as if startled I again bend down my head
Behind my books, and venture not to speak
To her, although I do remember former joy.
And as if heartless I work on all day
Not looking up nor round, because I fear
The great grief I shall see in that dark eye.
For she was once so lovely, my young wistfulness,
When all the flowers joyfully would bloom
For us, and birds were mocking our young grief.
But now the last bird sits there tucked away
Among the branches; through the narrow crack
Between the half-closed shutters falls the light
On us, who grieve in the deserted house.

Of the love named friendship

Light of my soul! I saw thee from afar
And always knew that thou at last would come; –
Words I have yet confided unto none
Go out from me like pale flames; – like a star

Deep in the blue, but brighter, lovelier,
I see framed in thy hair the shining face;
The mystery of much grief, but never hate
Dreams in thine eyes; – I always saw it, far.

Ik zal u zien, mijn Licht, zo zie gij mij:
In één zoet waas van gloed, waar ieder woord
Doorheenvlamt van de lippen en saamglijdt
Met andre tot één lichtende enigheid –
En elk van ons droomt in een glorie voort,
En andre glorie gaat ons stil voorbij.

7

Mijn god is enkel gloed en donkerheid,
Schoon om te zien, – een wonder te verstaan; –
Daar is niet één als Hij, – doch 'k zie u aan,
En waan dat gij Hemzelf op aarde zijt.

En dus heb ik mijn ziele u toegewijd,
Opdat ze in uwen gloed mochte vergaan;
En stil verteren, zonder klacht, voldaan
Met zulk een liefde en zulk een enigheid.

Zoals twee vlammen spelen in den nacht,
En nijgen naar elkaar met bleker gloor,
En trillen sneller in elkanders gloed, –
Tot bei opvlammend in de lucht, in 't zoet
Verenen beven, – dan, den nanacht door,
Brandt éne grote vlam, in kalme pracht.

8

O Man van Smarte met de doornenkroon,
O bleek bebloed gelaat, dat in den nacht
Gloeit als een grote, bleke vlam, – wat macht
Van eindloos lijden maakt uw beeld zo schoon?

Glanzende Liefde in enen damp van hoon,
Wat zijn uw lippen stil, hoe zonder klacht
Staart ge af van 't kruis, – hoe lacht gij soms zo zacht,
God van Mysterie, Gods bemindste Zoon!

I will see thee, my Light, so see thou me:
In one sweet haze of glow, through which each word
Flames from the lips, and joined together glides
With other ones and in one sheen unites –
And each of us dreams in a glory shared,
And other glory goes by silently.

7

My god is darkness and is glowing fire,
Beauteous to see, – a miracle to know; –
There is not one like Him, – but seeing you
I feel as if Himself on earth you are.

And therefore I have turned my soul to live
For you, that it may perish in your glow
And gently waste away, and never rue,
Fulfilled by such a union and such love.

As two flames that are playing in the night,
And bending towards each other's paler glow,
Trembling more swiftly in each other's heat, –
Till both, leaping up higher in their sweet
Union will quiver, – then, till break of day,
Burns one great flame in quiet splendour bright.

8

O Man of Sorrow with the crown of thorn,
Pale bloodstained countenance, which in the night
Glows like a great, pale flame, – what might
Of infinite suffering glorifies your form?

Radiant Love beneath a cloud of scorn,
How are your lips so still, while you resigned
Gaze from the cross, – how is your smile so kind,
God of deep Mystery, God's most-loved Son!

O Vlam van Passie in dit koud heelal!
Schoonheid van Smarten op deez' donkere aard!
Wonder van Liefde, dat geen sterfling weet!

Ai mij! ik hoor aldoor den droeven val
Der dropplen bloeds en tot den morgen staart
Hij me aan met grote liefde en eindloos leed.

1885

Cor Cordium

I

Ziel van mijn Ziel! Leven, dat in mij woont,
Veelnamige Mysterie, die ik noem
Mijn Ik, mijn Zelf, mijn Wezen, – die u toont
Altijd een andre, en uwen eigen doem
Spreekt op u zelve en dit mijn lichaam maakt
Het werktuig uwer woorden, 't instrument,
Dat gij bespeelt en maakt aan de aard bekend
Uw melodieën, dat aanstónds ontwaakt
Dit mensdom heinde en veer: – ú roep ik aan;
Opdat gij spreke en van mijn lippen drijv'
Lente van zang, die over de aard zal gaan,
En 'k thans niet mijn maar úwe woorden schrijv'.

II

'k Heb u altijd gezocht en trachtte altijd
Te luistren naar uw woorden; maar als een
Die staat aan 't strand der zee en hoort aldoor
Der waatren ruisen en het wijd en zijd
Breken der golven, en zijn voeten treên
Krakende schelpen; – en hij nijgt het oor,
Om in 't geluid te grijpen één geluid,
Omdat, als hij het hoort, hij zal verstaan
Ontzachbre wijsheid, zulke als de Natuur

O Flame of Passion in this cold vast All!
Beauty of Sorrows in this sombre world!
Wonder of Love, of which no mortals know!

Ah me! I grieve to hear the steady fall
Of drops of blood, and until dawn behold
Him gaze on me with love and endless woe.

Cor Cordium

I

Soul of my Soul! Life that within me dwells,
Many-named Mystery, which I call
My Ego, Self, my Essence, – thou who show'st
Thyself always another and wilt speak
Thy doom upon thyself, and make my body
Broadcast thy works and be the instrument
Which thou dost use so that the earth may hear
Thy melodies, and that mankind at once
Awakens near and far; – on thee I call,
That thou may'st speak, that from my lips may flow
Springtime of song, which shall pervade the earth,
And that I write not *my* words now, but thine.

II

I've always sought thee and have always tried
To listen to thy words; but like a man
Who stands on the sea-shore and ever hears
The roaring of the waters and the far and wide
Breaking of waves, and as he walks, his feet
Tread crunching shells; – and he will strain his ear
To grasp in all the weltering noise one sound,
Because, if he hears that, he'll understand
Tremendous wisdom, such as Nature will

Eens in een eeuw, aan één verkorene uur,
Meêgeeft, opdat die ze uitlegge en beduid'
Den grootste van die dán op aarde gaan; –
Maar vruchtloos: – zó hoorde ik in mijne ziel,
Van dat ik kind was en der wereld droom
Kleurde mijn ogen met zijn bonte beeld, –
Een heir van stemmen in mij, en ik hiel'
Mijn oren wakker in den nacht, vol schroom
Biddend, dat me úw geluid niet bleef verheeld.
O, als een kind, dat op een marktplaats dwaalt,
En roept zijn moeder, die hij daar verloor,
En schreit of eindlijk hem zijn moeder haalt,
En meent haar stem te vangen in zijn oor; –
Zoals dat kind, als moeder toch niet komt,
Zo schreide ik ook om u, die me alles zijt,
Moeder en meer dan die; – die 'k thans belijd
Liever dan mensen; – die u nóg vermomt,
Helaas! terwijl ik klaag en mijn geluid
Uitween in stroom van tonen en begeer
Alleen met u te zijn, in schoon verkeer
Van woorden, – tot uw hand mij de ogen sluit.

III

Wee mij! Ik had mijn oren moê gemaakt
Met luistren naar veel woorden. Ik verstond
De taal der mensen, wier geslachten gaan,
Rusteloos sprekende, als een karavaan
Van volkren. En iets was er dat ik vond
Van wat in bossen en op waatren waakt:
Toen was ik moede toen ik 't had verstaan.
En zoals een, die moede is van 't gepraat
Der stad en 't druk bedrijf langs markt en straat,
Gaat in het huis eens vriends, dat die tot hem
Vertrouwlijk spreke, met gedempte stem,
Onder 't gedempte lamplicht; of als een,
Die 't stads-raadhuis verlaat en 't lang geluid
Der luide stemmen in de hoge zaal: –
Hij treedt met vluggen tred door 't ruim portaal,

Give once in a hundred years to one blest hour,
That it interpret and explain that sound
To one, the greatest who then walks on earth; –
But listens vainly – so within my soul
Ever since, as a child, my eyes were charmed
By the bright-coloured dream that is the world, –
I heard a host of voices, and my ears
Were watchful in the night, as full of awe
I prayed thy voice might not be kept from me.
O, like a child that roams a market-place
Calling his mother who is lost to him,
– He cries with longing that she'll come at last
And thinks he caught her voice now in his ear; –
So, like that child, when mother does not come,
I've cried for thee, who art my one and all,
Mother and more than she – whom I do now
Avow dearer than humans; – thou who still,
Alas, hid'st from me while I moan and weep
For thee in streams of sound, as I desire
To be alone with thee, commune with thee
In words, – until thy hand shall close my eyes.

III

Woe's me! I'd made my ears so deeply tired
By listening to a flood of words. I heard
And understood the speech of men, who go
By generations, ever speaking, like a caravan
Of peoples. And something too, I had found
Of what in woods and on the waters dwells:
Then I was weary when I'd understood.
And like a man who's weary of the talk
Of town, the bustle of the squares and streets,
Goes to a friend's house, who will speak to him
In confidence, in a gentle tone of voice
Under a lamp's subdued light, or like one
Who leaves the town hall and the noisy sound
Of the loud voices in the lofty hall; –
He swiftly traverses the vestibule,

En daalt de trappen af en de stad door,
Naar een stil huis, dat in de voorstad staat,
En hij treedt in, wijl hij de straatdeur sluit,
En vindt in 't stil vertrek zijn liefste alleen,
En zij zegt zoete woordjes aan zijn oor,
En laat hem zitten, – wijl zij nederligt
Op haar satijnen sofa, – aan haar zij,
Op een laag stoeltjen, en hij legt zijn hoofd
Tegen haar aan, en zij kust gaarne 't licht
Der ogen hem en maakt rond hem gevlei
Van woorden, waarvan elk iets liefs belooft: –
Zó zocht 'k – o, man noch maagd tot vriend noch vrouw –
Maar ú alleen, die 'k wist dat meer zou zijn;
En beter dan een man zijn vriend kent, wou
'k O kennen, dat ik u ware en gij mijn'.
Toen werd mijn staêge taak steeds te verstaan
Elk ding dat van u kwam en uw schoon rijk;
En 'k zat met uw gedachten daaglijks aan,
En elk noemde uwen naam geduriglijk.
En uwe dromen zochten me als ik sliep,
En weefden voor mijn oog veelkleurgen schijn.
En verre stemmen zongen uit het diep,
Totdat de laatste toon mij wakker riep,
En 'k smeekte: 'och, dat die stem thans *niet* verdwijn'!'
Dan stonden mijn gedachten bij elkaar
In 't vale licht, en geen sprak onder hen,
En enklen weenden; en zij fluisterden
En zagen mij aan, droef, totdat een paar
Glimlachten door hun tranen heen, en 'k zei:
'Mijn lief! ik voel uw lachen over mij.'

Wee mij, gelijk de dageraad altijd
Een korte dag is, eer de regen komt,
Vroeg in den morgen, en de scheemring glijdt
Weer over de aarde en 't vooglenkoor verstomt
Tussen de bosjes, waar het nauw weerklonk: –
Zó was mijn vreugd slechts vreugdes dageraad,
Waar o zo droef een dag van leed op zonk: –
Want nóg trilde in mijn oren dóór, 't gepraat
Der mensen, en in mijn gezichten blonk

Descends the stairs and goes far through the town
Towards a quiet house in outer streets,
And he goes in and closes the front door,
And in the quiet room he finds his love alone,
And she whispers sweet nothings in his ear
And bids him sit, – while she lies down
On her silk sofa, – closely by her side
On a low chair, and as he lays his head
Leaning against her, she will gladly kiss
His eyes, envelop him in a fond mist
Of loving words, and each sweet promise holds: –
So did I seek – o, man nor maid, woman nor friend,
But thee alone who would, I knew, be more;
And, better than one knows one's friend, I wished
To know thee, that I might be thee, thou mine.
Then my fixed task became always to take
Each thing that came from thee and thy fair realm,
And daily I held converse with thy thoughts,
And each would say thy name continually.
Thy dreams would come to me during my sleep,
And weave before my eye colourful light.
And far-off voices chanted from the deep
Until the closing note would waken me
And I'd implore: 'may that voice leave me not!'
And then my thoughts would close together stand
In the grey light, and none of them would speak,
A few were weeping, and they'd whisper then
Regarding me so sadly, till a few
Would gently smile through tears, and I would say:
'My love, I feel thee smiling over me.'

Ah, woe is me: – as dawn will always break
To be a short day only, till the rain
Comes early in the morning, and the dusk
Once more will glide over the earth, bird song
Falls silent in the trees, though scarce begun:-
So was my joy then merely joy's brief dawn,
Whereon so sorrowful a day would sink: –
For still my ears were buzzing with the talk
Of people, and my visions still would shine

De lichte erinring van der mensen daad,
En in úw woorden waande ik telken keer
Hún woord te horen, en elk nieuw gezicht
Zag 'k vol gestalten staan, als die 'k weleer
Bewegen zag en lachen in het licht
Eens aardsen dags; – wee mij! de bitterheid
Des levens proefde ik bitter in mijn mond,
En uw gedachten, die gij tot mij zondt
Als troosters, haatte ik en heb zeer beschreid
Dit lichaam, dat zo droef op aarde stond.
Want 't was me als had een vreemd man in mijn ziel
U-zelf gedood en stuurde, uit gruwbren spot,
Zijn boden mij, opdat ik nederviel,
In ijdle aanbidding, voor een vreemden God.
Toen maakte ik den nacht bleek met mijnen hoon,
En riep uzelf tegen uzelven aan: –
En 'k zag, lijkkleurig, mijn gedachten staan,
Met wijd-ope ogen, als ontwaakte doôn.

IV

Toen zocht ik op de wegen van mijn ziel
Al uw gedachten, die daar dag en nacht
Spreken van u: – zó als men soms mocht zien
Feestgangers, gaande naar een grote stad,
Bij troepen op den heirweg; al die liên
Maakten verward geluid, en lieten pracht
Van kleurge mantels, of fluwelen kiel,
Of pluimhoed pronken in het zonlicht, dat
Bij vollen middag van den hemel viel; –
Of anders: pelgrims, die in grauwe pij,
De armen gekruist, met zware stappen gaan
Achter elkander, in het koude licht
Eens vroegen morgens: – zo gaan, droef of blij,
Al uw gedachten altijd af en aan,
En zijn altijd nabij voor mijn gezicht: –
Al dezen vroeg ik en zij spraken mij
Van al uw deugden, groot en wonderbaar,
Want die te zeggen, dat was al hun eer;

With the bright memories of human deeds,
And in thy words each time I'd seem to hear
Their words, and in each vision I would see
A throng of figures, as in former times
I had seen moving, laughing in the light
Of earthly day; – woe's me! the bitterness
Of life then tasted bitter in my mouth;
The very thoughts that thou wouldst send to me
As comforters, I hated, and I have bemoaned
This body that so sadly dwelt on earth.
Because I felt as if a strange man had
Killed thee within my soul, and mockingly
Sent me his messengers, that I might kneel
In vain worship before an idol-god.
Then I made night grow pallid with my scorn,
And called upon thyself against thyself: –
And saw, corpse-wan, my thoughts before me stand,
With eyes wide-open, like awakened dead.

IV

Then on the pathways of my soul I sought
The many thoughts which there by day and night
Tell me of thee: – as one sometimes might see
Revellers going to a famous town
In crowds along the highway; all those men
Made confused noises, and they wore
Splendidly coloured cloaks, or velvet smocks,
Or plumed hats gorgeous in the sunlight, which
At highest noon was shining from the sky; –
Or otherwise: pilgrims in dark-grey garb,
Arms folded, who, striding with heavy tread
Go following each other in the cold
Light of early morning – so, sad or blithe,
Do all thy thoughts always go to and fro
And always are near-by before my sight.
All these I questioned, and they spoke to me
Of all thy virtues, great and wonderful,
Because in telling me they took great pride;

En ik besloot hun woorden altegaar
In mijn geheugen en dacht telkens meer
Te kennen u, dien 'k andren openbaar.
En toen kwam er een tijd, waarin ik dacht
Te weten wie gij zijt; en 'k zag uw beeld
's Daags voor mij, en werd wakker in den nacht,
Van grote vreugde, omdat ik 't half verheeld,
In droom ontwaarde. En weken na elkaar
Heb ik mijzelf kinderlijk-blij gespeeld
Met dat vals beeld, dat 'k zelf had voortgebracht.

Wee mij! Toen hoorde ik, zittende in mijn huis,
De stemmen der gedachten weer in mij:
Zij kwamen traag van verre, als het geruis
Dat de wind maakt tussen een huizenrij:
Maar 't was een vreemd geluid, als iemand hoort,
Die van de Noordstreek naar het Zuiden gaat,
Bij andre volken, en hoort woord na woord
Spreken door wandlaars, in een vreemde straat,
Zuidlijke talen: – en ik zag, en ziet!
Diep in de scheemring van mijn ziel bewoog
Een drom gestalten, als ik somtijds zag
Gaan op de bruggen, als ik 't huis verliet,
En op een gracht liep, waar de mist langs toog,
Op een Novembermorgen: de wind lag
Roerloos over de stad: zo was 't in mij.
En 'k zag ze naadren en ik hoorde 't blij
Geluid der stemmen en mijn oor vernam, –
Wee mij, dat het vernam! – elk woord dat kwam
Van u, helaas! als al wat in mij spreekt: –
Van u, maar niet van hem, dien 'k had gemaakt,
't Beeld dat ik had gemaakt in mensenwaan,
't Prentje, waarvan 'k mijzelf had voorgepreekt,
Dat gij het waart, en waar 'k om had verzaakt
Uzelf, *mijn* zelf, dat niemand kán verstaan:
Van u, mijn onbewuste Zelf, mijn Ziel
Der ziel, Leven mijns levens, lamploos Licht,
Dat in schone geheimnis altijd gloort,
En brandt in 't duister, daar het eens in viel,
Deez' aard, deez' stof, die voor mijn blind gezicht

And I enshrined their words, yea all of them
Within my mind, thinking that each time more
I knew thee, whom to others I reveal.
And then there came a time when I believed
I did know who thou art; I saw thy form
Before me in the daytime, and at night
I'd wake with joy, as faintly, in a dream
I had perceived it. And for weeks on end
I played myself childishly glad, and pleased
With that false image I myself had made.

Woe's me! Then, one day, as I sat at home,
I once more heard the voices of my thoughts:
They slowly came from far-off, like the sound
The wind makes round the houses in a street:
But 'twas a strange sound, such as one may hear
Going from Northern regions to the South
Mid other nations, and one hears the words
Spoken by people walking on strange streets
In southern tongues: – and then I saw and, look!
Deep in the gloaming of my soul there moved
A throng of figures, as I sometimes saw
Crossing the bridges as I left the house
And walked along the water, where the fog
Moved one November morning; the wind lay
Stirless over the town: so was my mind.
I saw them drawing nearer, heard the glad
Sound of the voices, and my ear discerned, –
Woe's me, that it discerned! – each word that came
From thee, alas! as all that in me speaks: –
From thee, but not from him whom I had made,
The image I had made fancying human-wise,
The picture which I'd made myself believe
Was thee, for which I had betrayed
Thyself, *my* self, whom none can understand:
Thee, my unconscious Self, Soul of my soul,
Life of my life, thee, lampless Light
Which in beautiful mystery always glows
And burns in darkness into which it fell,
This earth, this dust, which to my poor blind sight

U overschijnt, wien alle schijnsel hoort.
Vergeef! ik kan niet weten wie gij zijt,
Ik zie het eind niet van wat eeuwig blijft:
't Bewuste onthult het onbewuste niet: –
Wij leven en vergaan, gij zijt altijd;
Maar met u blijft wat ge ons in 't harte drijft,
En al wat we, u ter eer, zeggen in 't Lied.

V

Toen zag ik ene, een vrouw, wier diepste ziel
Lag in haar ogen als een dageraad,
En lucht vol tinten die weerspiegeld viel
In een stil water: – en als een, die staat
Stil op een heide, als heel de heide gloeit,
Purper in 't licht: hij voelt op zijn gelaat
Den weerschijn beven, die in golven vloeit
Onder de heemlen, en hij waant te zijn
Een deel dier ruimte, een kind van de atmosfeer
Rondom, en de aarde, die op eens ontbloeit: –
Zo zag 'k mijzelf bewegen in den schijn
Harer nabijheid, en ik dacht niet meer
Te zijn, bij haar, dan een bloem is in 't licht,
Waardoor zij bloem werd, dan het spiegelbeeld
Der maan in d'oceaan, dat nachtlijks speelt
Onder de golven, doch 't beschaamd gezicht
Daar niet kon schuilen zonder d'oceaan;
En toen vergat 'k, helaas, dat gij altijd
Blijft die gij zijt, al drijft der mensen waan
Met al de winden: en ik loog mij voor
Dat het úw wil was dat ik u verloor,
En dat u vinden was in háár vergaan,
En dat de Liefde meer was dan gij zijt!
En gij zaat stil in de verborgenheid
Uws raads, en zondt drom van gedachten aan,
Als slaven, dragende veel schats, belaân
Met edel goud van wijsheid, en sieraad
Van kostbre woorden, en brocaat gewaad
Van koninklijke hoogheid; en elkeen

Does outshine thee, from whom all radiance flows.
Forgive! I cannot fathom who thou art.
I see no end to what forever stays.
No conscious thought reveals Un-consciousness; –
We live and perish, thou dost ever stay;
But with thee stays what thou lay'st in our heart,
And all that, in thy praise, singing we say.

V

Then I beheld a girl whose deepest soul
Lay in her eyes like an arising dawn,
A many-coloured sky whose mirrored form
Showed in still water: – and like one who stands
Still on a moorland, when the heather glows
Purple in sunlight: on his face he feels
The trembling radiance which surging flows
Under the heavens, and believes he is
Part of that space, offspring of Atmosphere
Around him and of Earth suddenly blossoming: –
So did I see myself move in the sheen
Of her near presence, thought myself no more
Before her than a flower is in the light
Through which it blooms, than the moon's mirror-shape
Seen in the ocean, which all night will play
Under the waves, but could not hide away
Her bashful face, if Ocean were not there.
And I forgot, alas, that thou always
Remain'st the one thou art, though human thought
Blows with the winds: and I deceived myself,
Pretending I had lost thee by thy will,
That finding thee was: losing myself in her,
Believing Love was greater than thou art!
And thou wert seated still in the arcane
Depth of thy council, sending throngs of thoughts
Like slaves bearing much treasure, loads
Of noble gold of wisdom, splendid gems
Of costly words, and garments of brocade
Of regal state, and then would every one

Van uw gedachten ging met hare saam:
Twee schone wolken, woelende ondereen; –
En 'k zag ze in groepen en bij tweeën treên,
En hoorde aldoor uw naam en haren naam.
En de een, de andere ontmoetend, kuste haar,
Zodat de lucht licht werd van vreugde om hen.
En hen te aanzien onthulde ons wonderbaar
Der Liefde dienst en ceremoniën.
Toen bloeiden onze kussen in den nacht,
Als tweeling-bloemen, nijgend naar elkaar,
Die saam op één steel beven en dan zacht
Elkaar omsluiten in hún nacht van 't jaar.
En om ons heen bewoog de duisternis,
Als om twee vlammen, bevend te vergaan
Iedere in de andre, en die dan roerloos staan,
Als één vlam brandend tot het uchtend is.
Wee mij! wee ieder die zich zelf ontviel!
Want het verlangen naar zijn zelf zal dra
Gelijk een sterk man woeden in zijn ziel, –
En wie verhoort dan 't roepen om gena?
Want de gedachten die hij 't liefste had
Zullen als droeve slaven schreiend staan,
En klagend vragen of hij hen vergat,
Die zoveel schoons hem hebben aangedaan.
Zij zullen 't huis bevolken in zijn droom,
En, sombre stoeten, maken zulk misbaar,
Dat hij in slaap zal zeggen: koom, o koom!
En de armen oopnen naar die droeve schaar.
En als de nachtlamp walmt en geler brandt,
Des ochtends, vliên zij, en hij zal misschien,
Met dromende ogen, naast het ledekant,
Een enkle zitten en zacht schreien zien.
En 't zal hem zijn – wee mij, dat ik het weet! –
Gelijk 't een kind is, dat de moeder schonk
Speelgoed: een popje en kleertjes, en het kleedt
Lief popjen aan en dost lief popje in pronk
Van jurkje en fraai sieraad en mint het zéér,
Zó dat het slaapt met popje en telkens meer
Voor popje lief wordt; maar op 't laatst vergeet
Vriendjes en moeder-zelf, – tot 't op een keer

Of thy profoundest thoughts go forth with hers:
Two lovely clouds, mingling in whirling dance.
I saw them how they trod in groups and pairs
And kept hearing thy name joined with her name.
And one, meeting the other, kissed her then,
So that the sky grew bright with joy in them.
And watching them wonderfully revealed
To us Love's service and her ceremonies.
Then did our kisses blossom in the night
As might twin flowers bending each to each
Tremble on one stem and would gently then
Embrace each other in their year's one night.
And all around us both the darkness moved
As round two flames that trembling want to melt
Each in the other, and then moveless stand
As one flame burning until dawn has come.
Woe's me! Woe's each one who forsook himself!
Because the longing for his self will soon
Be raging like a strong man in his soul, -
And when he cries for mercy, who shall hear?
Because the thoughts that were most dear to him
Will stand before him weeping like sad slaves,
Plaintively asking whether he forgot
Them, who had given him such loveliness.
They'll people all the house, and in his dream,
Sombre processions, they will clamour so
That in his sleep he'll tell them: come, o come!,
And open wide his arms to that sad throng.
And when the night-lamp fumes and yellower burns
At dawn, they'll flee from him, and then, maybe,
He'll see a lone one sitting by his bed
With dreaming eyes and weeping quietly,
And he will be – woe's me that I should know! –
Like a young child to whom her mother gave
Toys: a little doll and clothes, and she will dress
Her dolly lovingly, deck it in choice
Of little frocks and precious gems, and love
Sweet dolly dearly, sleep with it in bed,
Grow ever fonder of it, but at last
Forget friends and mother herself – until

Die moeder dood vindt; – zoals dan dat kind
Schreit om zijn moeder en haar eenzaam leed,
En dat het popje liefhad boven haar: –
Zó zal hij schreien, die zijn Zelf vergeet,
En meer dan Zelf liefde van mensen mint,
Alsof die meer dan 's levens Leven waar'.

VI

Daar leeft geen ándre God! Gij zijt alleen.
Der wereld heil moog' einden in geween,
Hij die in u gelooft smaakt eeuwge vreugd.
U voelen is geluk, u zoeken deugd;
U kennen was altoos der grootsten droom:
Al hun gebed, dat úw koninkrijk koom',
Want wie u mint, bemint de wereld niet;
Werelden worden en vergaan – gij blijft:
En met u blijft wat ge ons in 't harte drijft,
En al wat we, u ter eer, zeggen in 't Lied.

27–31 July 1886

She finds her mother dead; – as then that child
Cries over mother and her lonely grief
And having held her doll dearer than her –
Só will he cry who will forget his Self
And more than Self hold dear the human love,
As if that could surpass the Life of life.

VI

There lives no óther God! Thou only art.
The world's delight may end in deep distress,
Who trusts in thee receives eternal joy.
To seek thee is virtue – feel thee, happiness,
To know thee was of old the greatests' dream,
All that they prayed was that 'thy kingdom come'.
Whoever loves thee, loves not the world's way;
Worlds grow and perish – thou dost ever stay:
And with thee stays what thou lay'st in our heart,
And all that, in thy praise, singing we say.

Jonge liefde

1

Ik zal mijn lief veel schone verzen sturen
Die om haar heen staan en haar daaglijks dienen,
Haar lieve beelden bootsen, nooit-gezienen,
Blij-ruchtig lachen door haar eenzame uren.
Als meisjes zullen ze om haar heen borduren,
Heel 'n school, eenzelfd patroon, waarop zij vliên en
Zich naadren zien zal lieven van stramien en
Bont zijwerk in bosschaadjige figuren.
Zó zal geen vorst zijn liefste kind omstoeten
Met vrome en trouwe, vorstlijke dienaren,
Als ik mijn kind met vrome en prachtge woorden.
Die zullen met haar gaan als zij langs boorden
Van stille waatren gaat, en 's nachts omwaren
Met stille lampen van eerbiedge groeten.

2

Want ik ben bij u, lief! Als ge in den nacht
Roeit onder 't groen en weinig sterren ziet,
Dan ben 'k in 't bootje en op het water niet,
En niet in manelicht of sterrenwacht.

Maar 'k ben in krekelzang en vogelklacht,
In 't bosjesgroen als er de wind door schiet,
In 't riet dat wuift waartussen 't water vliet,
In 't kabblend klanken om uw riemslag zacht.

Ik ben in al wat luidt en klankt in 't rond,
Al wat geluid maakt dat een mensenmond
Kan maken als hij dichterlippen heeft.
Dáarin ben 'k bij u, lief. Want mijne ziel is al
Wat klinkt in 't bos en op den waterval,
Al wat onsterfelijk in woorden leeft.

Young love

1

I'll send my love full many beauteous verses
That will stand round her and will daily serve her
And show her lovely pictures, never seen,
Merrily laughing through her lonely hours.
Like girls they'll sit around, embroidering
– A school of girls – one pattern, where she'll marvel
At fleeing and approaching figures: – lovers
Encompassed by gay groups in pleasant groves.

No prince will so surround his dearest one
With loyal and devoted princely pages
As I'll surround my dear with fair, devoted words.
They will go with her as she skirts the banks
Of quiet waters, and at night surround her
With quiet lamps of reverent saluting.

2

For I am with you, love! When in the night
You row under green trees and a sparse star,
Then I'm not in the boat, nor on the mere,
Nor among guardian stars or in moonlight.

But in the cricket's chirp, birds' plaint ashore,
Among the trees' leaves shaken by the wind,
In reeds that wave along the margin's bend,
In ripples lapping where you stir your oar.

I am in all that rings and sings around,
In all those things that will bring forth a sound
That quickens music on a poet's lips.
There I am with you, love. My soul is all
That sounds in woods and on the waterfall,
All that in singing words immortal lives.

3

Leer nu met vrome eerbiedige gedachten,
Mijn vers, dat kind dat ik zo liefheb naken.
Mijn handen zijt ge en moogt haar haren raken,
Gij zijt mijn lippen, kus haar lippen zacht en
Spreek lieve vragen en verliefde klachten.
Mijn oren zijt gij: blijf gestadig waken:
Zij spreekt luid als zij slaapt en zal niet laken
In droom hem waar haar lippen 's daags naar lachten.
Gij zult gelukger dan uw meester wezen,
Mijn vers; want gij zult aldoor bij haar blijven.
Als zij u leest zult ge in haar ogen lezen
't Vers dat ze op mij maakt, maar nooit op wil schrijven.
En gij zult nooit zo dwaas als ik voor dezen
Haar liefste lachen angstig van u drijven.

Herfstavond

Op 't donkre buiten
Boomkruinen ruisen:
Stormwolken drijven:
In 't lamplicht huis en
Voor donkre ruiten,
Zit 'n dromend beeld
Woorden te schrijven,
En 't kruinenruisen,
En 't wolkendrijven,
Staat, een geluid, in
Schrift gepenseeld.

3

Learn then, with earnest and revering mind,
My verse, to draw near her I hold so dear.
My hands you are, and you may stroke her hair,
You are my lips – kiss her lips gently, and
Beg lovingly and tenderly lament.
My ears you are, so always watchful stay:
She'll speak when sleeping and won't reprimand,
When dreaming, him her lips smiled on by day.
You'll be more lucky than your master is,
My verse; because you'll always be with *her.*
For, as she reads, you're reading in her eyes
The verse she'll make on me, but never write.
And you'll not foolishly, like me before,
Drive her sweet smile away from you in fright.

Autumn evening

In the sombre park
Tree-crowns are sighing:
Storm-clouds are floating:
In the lamp-lit mansion
By a window, dark,
Sits a dreaming form,
Thinks words he is writing;
And the tree-crowns' sighing,
The dark clouds' floating
Stay, now a sound, in
Written form.

De natuurlijke aarde, 7

Een donker woud –
Een stille wel –
Daarin geschouwd –
Was ik dat wel?

Mij wil niet laten
Het vreemd vizioen:
Een bleek gelaat en
Een groen plantsoen.

Van woud en hemel
Lag het omloofd,
Van ogen-wemel
Doorblonken 't hoofd.

Ogen, twee donkren
Poelen gelijk –
Wat glom dat flonkren –
Waar nam 't de wijk? –

Wie voert mij weer
Langs de oude straat?
Ik bukte er neer
Naar 't bleek gelaat.

In 't donkre woud,
In stille wel,
Heb ik 't geschouwd –
Was ik dat wel?

October 6 1894

The natural earth, 7

A dark wood –
A quiet well –
And therein showed –
Was that myself?

It will not leave me,
The strange thing seen:
A pale face,
And foliage green.

In wood and skies
The head lay framed,
And shining eyes
Therein gleamed.

The eyes were seeming
Dark pools, they shone –
How clear their gleaming –
Where is it gone? –

Who will once more
Lead me those ways?
I bent down, lower,
Towards the pale face.

In the dark wood,
The quiet well,
The vision showed –
Was that myself?

Nieuwe neiging

6

't Hangen naar schoonheid is een groot geneugt –
Als in een droom wen een wit meisjeskleed
Vliedt en nog wenkt in donker groen en treedt
Dan in een open, en mijn voet verheugd

Wil volgen, tot een lach klinkt en niet weet
'k Opeens vanwaar, want zacht, vol droevge vreugd,
Word 'k wakker, zó dat lach en luistring heugt
Den dag door en ik traag mijn droom vergeet;

Zo de gedachten als een lieflijk beeld
Zich toont en 't volgen op zijn scheemrend spoor
Zoet wordt den schoonheid zeer lievenden man.
De morgen gaat, de middag, en aldoor
Vliedt en verschijnt daar mijn gedacht meê speelt,
Tot de nacht komt en 'k lach en schrei ervan.

7

Zwol niet een aar zo op den akker, hart,
Van zon en sap totdat uit mager groen
Het gouden korrelhoofd in ruigen baard
Zoetlijk opneeg naar lauwer winden zoen?

Zwol niet het blauw totdat het zonhoofd werd
Zwart van zijn blaken en afgrondlijk glôen?
Blonk niet, een donkre vrouw wier schoonheid zwart
Blonk, d'aard, – als parels groot in water doen?

Zwol zo ons lijf niet, dat een land gelijk,
Open lag tot in 't vochtge hart voor zon?
Zwol er geen goud de rijpe ronding rijk?
Blonk 't licht niet zwart dat géén doorgronden kon?
't Donkre geheim van droom afgrondelijk
Daar 't licht in laait waar 't witte lijf rond spon? –

New trend

6

Longing for beauty is a great delight –
As in a dream when a girl's glinting dress
Fleeing still beckons in dark green; she treads
Then in a clearing; happily my feet

Will follow, till a laugh rings out, and yet
From where I know not; gently, with sad joy
I wake, so that both laugh and listening stay
All day: my dream, which slowly I forget;

So are my thoughts when an endearing shape
Appears, and following its fleeting trace
Grows sweet for the lover of loveliness.
The morning goes, the afternoon – always
Flees and appears what through my thinking plays,
Till the night comes; it makes me smile and weep.

7

Did not an ear thus swell in fields, my heart,
That grew of sun and sap till from thin green
The golden corn-head in its hairy beard
Sweetly arose, to meet the winds' warm kiss?

Swelled not the blue until the sun-head grew
Black with its blazing and engulfing glow?
Gleamed not, a dusky girl whose beauty gleamed
Darkly, the earth, as pearls in water do?

Swelled not our body so, which, like a field,
Its dewy heart laid open to the sun?
Swelled not to gold its richly rounded yield?
Glowed not the light coal-black, that's plumbed by none?
Dark mystery of an engulfing dream
In which light blazed where white the body spun?

Sterren I

1

Staat ge op het achterdek geleund voorover aan de
    verschansing,
Volgt er de fonklende voor die de kiel door 't donkere
    water
Snijdende toog: doorzwiert fosforische blauwing
Sparklend de schroef tot de sterren dien hemel doorflonkren
Sproeiende in 't melk-licht diep: opeens stijgt de romp op
    een zeegolf,
Daalt en stort neer in een dal maar verlaat het om hoger te
    stijgen:–
Duizling bevangt bij die leegte en die plotslinge wijking
U die daar staat – en de schroef holt door, haar geratel
Ruist over 't sterrengeglim dat vervloeit in de scheemrende
    kolken –
Wanhoop vult u en lust met uw lichaam te dempen
Chaos en 't leeg van dien wrakkig-geslagenen hemel:–
Zo, somtijds, aangreep mij 't heelal van een geest als ik hol zag
Ruimten waar eens zo vervoerende sterren mij blonken.

23 July 1898

2

Ziet ge onder 't kleed van een badende vrouw
De tedere borstjes bewegen –
Uit die golving lief en levens-lauw
Beeft u de schoonheid tegen

Die uit de golvende lucht en zee
In onvoltooide lijnen
Op vorm belust aanspoelde en deê
Dat zoete beeld opschijnen,

Stars I

1

Standing on the ship's stern you lean forward upon the
   railing,
Follow the sparkling groove that the keel through darkened
   water
Foaming cuts, as through its phosphoric blue the propeller
Swirls till that watery sky is a-glitter with stars
Sprayed in the milk-pale depths; – but then the hull rears on a
   sea-swell,
Sinks to crash down in a gulf, but leaves it to soar yet
   higher; –
Dizzy, you reel at that void and that sudden dropping
As you, clinging, stand – the propeller runs on, its rattle
Roars o'er the stars' glimmer now melting in dusky
   whirlpools –
Desperate now, you desire to damp with your body
Chaos, the void of that reeling crumbling heaven:-
So, sometimes, would the world of a mind perturb me,
   as I saw hollow
Spaces, where once such radiant stars had inspired me.

2

Under the dress of a bathing girl
See, the tender breasts are moving –
From that lovely living surge
Trembling beauty meets you

Which from the surging sea and sky
In still burgeoning line,
Wanting shape, was washed ashore
And made that sweet form shine,

Dat schone beeld dat lijnen-rein
De schoonheid bei van zee en lucht
Belichaamt en mij toont – O pijn! –
Vermoeden laat ik zucht.

o Schoon beeld even door het kleed verhulde,
Uw borsten liggen rond
In de zo vol gevulde
Lap die ge u losjes bondt.

Gij staat voor 't zomers blauw,
Voor 't waters groen;
Uw lijnen fonkel-gauw,
Uw kleuren vlammen-koen.

Uw armen bliksem-blank
Slaan om uw hoofd, ai mij!
Ik hoor van zon een klank,
Van zee een schrei…

28–29 July 1898

De Kristaltwijg: Epiloog

Nu tot mijzelf
Keer ik en vind den Knaap
Die langs de grachten ging:
Zijn bedeesdheid
Groeide te zéér in hem.

Wanneer in donker
De sterren glansden,
En zijn lippen, geheven
Naar hun geglinster,
Woorden fluisterden,
Voelde zijn hart zich
Een bloem, geopend,
Offerend geur.

That lovely form whose perfect line
Shows me the sheen of sea and sky
Embodied, and I feel – O pain –
A stirring – breathe a sigh.

O lovely form just by the wrap concealed
Your breasts lie round
In the so fully filled
Scarf which you loosely bound.

You stand before summer's blue,
Before waters green,
Your lines sparkling through,
Your colours flaming, keen.

Your arms lightning-white
Fling round your head, ah me!
Hear how the sunlight rings,
How cries the sea...

Towards their glinting,

The Crystal Twig: Epilogue

Now I return
To myself and find the youth
Who walked by the town canals:
His shyness
Grew too greatly in him.

When in darkness
The stars were gleaming,
And his lips then, raised
Towards their glinting,
Would whisper words,
His heart would feel
A flower, opened,
Offering fragrance.

Toen tussen mensen
Zijn liedren klonken,
En hun bewondring,
Gewillige hulde,
Liefhebbend juichte,
Speelde zijn hand door zijn warre haren –
Aarzelend lachte bescheidenheid door zijn vreugddronken
blik.

o Instrument van die menslijke harten: bespeelde
Zacht hij niet eerst, toen luider, uw eindloos orgel? –
Voer op de zee naar het land van de menigten,
Leide aan de scheepsverschansing het oor te luistren:
't Lange gedreun, het kortklotsend gebreek aan den steven,
't Fluiten van wind door 't touwwerk, roep en bevelsklank

Op in het want, uit den mast, van man tot man, en in 't
donker
Preevlend gebed voor een dode en een plomp van een plank in
de golven –
o, En 't gespeel, in het ruim, in de hut, het verliefde gelispel:

Knaap die in spel tussen d'afgrond van hemel en aarde zijn spel
dreef.

Ach, instrument van de menslijke harten: de steden
Blonken elektrisch verlicht: hoe de volten krioelden.
Dondrende en flonkrende slang sneed de trein door streken,

Gaarden en hellingen langs waar het landhuis gloorde;
Dan door den nacht, op de donkre rivier waar 't water
Klotste op de pont en de stem aan ons oor als van ver klonk.

Golvende grond ontdeinde rondom: de prairie.
Soms het karkas van een paard: op de kim heel den avond
het weerlicht.
Binnen in 't rijdende huis in het licht de idylle, o liefste,
Van uw slapende hoofd in het korengoud van uw haren,
En ik, Prins uit het sprookje, die nederbukkend ze kuste.

When among people
His songs were ringing,
And they, admiring
With willing homage
Lovingly rejoiced,
Then his hand would ruffle his tousled hair –
Hesitantly diffidence smiled through his overjoyed gaze.

O instrument of those human hearts, did he not
Softly at first, then more loudly, sound your endless organ? –
Sailed oversea to the land of the multitudes,
Laid his ears to listen, leaning on the ship's railing
To the long-drawn roar, the short splashing crash on the prow,
The whistling of wind through the rigging, call and
    command-shout
High up aloft, from the mast, from man to man, and in the
    darkness
Muttering prayer for a dead man, then the plunge of a plank in
    the waves –
O, and the dallying, down in the hold, the cabin, the love-sick
    lisping:
Youth who, playing between heaven's and earth's abyss,
    pursued his pleasure.

Ah, instrument of the human hearts: the cities
Glittered in electric light: how the crowds were swarming!
A thundering, glittering snake, the train cut through
    landscapes
Skirting gardens and slopes where the mansion glowed;
Then through the night, on the dark river, where the water
Splashed on the ferry, the voice by our ear would seem far
    away –
Undulating land then opened around: the prairie.
Sometimes a horse's carcase would show; all night the hori-
    zon flashed with lightning.
Inside the rolling house, in the light, was the idyll, o dearest,
Of your sleeping head in the corn-gold of your hair,
And I, Prince of the fairy-tale, who bending over you,
    kissed it.

Dan waar de Geldvorst woonde, op de grens van die
   wereld,
Wetten te sterk, die zijn bruid de roodlokkige roofde, –

Weelde uit wereldsteden glom verdorven,
Weelde van goud, juwelen, ontblote vrouwen,
Paarden geleid onder 't vorstelijk dek als prinsen,
Weelde van slaven: de zwarte vrouw in 't wit mousseline,

Die, mijn raam langs, 's avonds den zwarten man zocht,

Weelde van kwaad en leed: de mesties loerend aan 't
   bergpad,
De arme Indiaan in het veld, en de Mexicaan zijn verhuis-
   boel
Ladend op 't hoofd van zijn vrouw en dan handen in
   broekzakken, fluitend.

Wee, instrument van de menslijke harten, hoe speelde ik
Zacht in mezelf, als de reizende prediker 't klokketouw
   luidde
En, met weinig armen, ik in de schaamle kapel trad,
Luider als 't land ik doorreed met duitsen koopman–

Kwam van Oud-Mexico, voerde sigaren rond in zijn huif-
   kar, –
Tussen de bergen het luidst als mijn paard zacht stapte
En 'k in het dorp den langbaardigen mijner vond bij den
   oven.

Tussen de bergen – fonkelden sterren ooit zo?
Klonk ooit menswoord groot als van mijn langbaardigen
   mijner? –

Want in de stilte tussen de bergen vond ik,
Vond een, daaglijks arbeidende onder de aarde,
En die toch begreep dat ik blij naar die sterren opzag,
Toch zijn land gedacht en vriendlijk 't mijne,
Want zijn moeder, zei hij, was ginds geboren.

Then to that world's border, where the Money-monarch
    lived,
The law-defying one, who had captured his red-haired
    bride, –
Luxury from the world's cities wickedly glittered,
Wealth of gold and jewels and half-nude women,
Horses led under regal cloth, like princes,
Abundance of slaves: the black woman dressed in white
    muslin
Passing under my window at night, seeking the black man she
    wanted,
Abundance of evil and suffering: The mestee who lurked by
    the hill-track,
The poor Indian in the field, the Mexican on the move,

His belongings loaded on his wife's back, and he hands in
    pockets, whistling.

Ah, instrument of the human hearts, how my music
Softly sang in myself, when the travelling preacher rang
    the bell,
As with a few more people, I entered the humble chapel;
It sang more loudly as I drove through the land with a
    German merchant –
Come from Old-Mexico, hawking cigars from his
    tilt-cart, –
Loudest among the mountains as my horse ambled gently
Where I found the long-bearded miner in the village by his
    stove.

Among the mountains – did ever stars glitter so brightly?
Was ever a man's word great like that of my long-bearded
    miner? –

For, in the stillness among the mountains I found,
Found one daily labouring underground,
And who yet understood my joyful gaze towards those stars,
Yet remembered his country, and kindly spoke of mine,
For his mother, he said, had been born yonder.

o Instrument van de menslijke harten: uw snaren,
Eindloos vele, zijn toch zo schoon geschapen,
Dat zij in één toon saam hun klank verenen.
Liefde van mens tot mens: – vond weergekomen
Ik niet mijn liefde en speelde op 't eindloos orgel,
Zong tot ik gans mijn ziel, al mijn gedachten,
Weg had gespeeld voor den Vriend, mijzelf gans ledig.

Toen tot mijzelf
Keerde ik en zocht den Knaap
Die langs de grachten ging: –
Zijn bedeesdheid
Groeide te zéér in hem. –

Heb ik aan het zeestrand niet haar gevonden
Die mij een Wereld was?
Is als uit de zee niet
Mij opgerezen
Een nieuwe wereld,
Totdat om dit rustoord
Zich de aarde spreidde? –
Welfde de hemel
Niet over ons?

Hoe heb ik liefgehad
Elk ding, elk mens –
En de dingen-liefde, en de liefde voor mensen,
Elk van die had in zich
Een strijd, een haat.

En ik peilde mijzelf,
En de strijd
Was in mij,
En de haat, onverganklijk,
Met mij geboren.

En de dingen-liefde
En de liefde voor mensen,
Elke deed groeien in mij
Een bedeesdheid; –
En mijn hart slonk.

O, instrument of the human hearts: your strings
Endlessly many, are yet formed in such beauty,
That together joined they sing one sound:
Love from one to another: did I not on my return
Find my love and played on the endless organ,
Sang till all my soul and all my thoughts
I had spent on the Friend, sung myself empty.

Then I returned
To myself and sought the youth
Who walked by the town canals: –
His shyness
Grew too greatly in him.

Did I not on the sea-shore find her
Who was a World for me?
Did not, as if from the sea
For me arise
A new world,
Till round this abode of peace
The earth unfolded? –
Was not the heavens'
Dome over us?

How I have loved
Each thing, each person –
And the love of things, and the love of people,
Each of them bore within it
A conflict, a hate.

And I fathomed myself,
And the conflict
Was in myself,
And the hate, imperishable,
Was born with me.

And the love of things
And the love of people
Each caused to grow within me
A shyness; –
And my heart shrank.

Maar nu tot mijzelf
Keerde ik, en vond den Knaap
Die langs de grachten ging,
En nu tot dien Knaap
Zeide ik dit woord: ja waarlijk,
Uw bedeesdheid groeide te zéér in u.

Want die gij liefhebt en die u bedeesd doen zijn,
Ding en mens, mens en ding,
Zij zijn eeuwig.
En de liefde die in u is
En die u bedeesd doet zijn,
Zij is eeuwig.
Maar gij alleen hebt het niet gezien.

Gij hadt in de dingen lief, in de mensen lief,
Het niet-Eeuwige.
Daarin is strijd en de haat die onmachtig maakt,
Daarin is Dood.
Maar nu tot het Eeuwige kom dat daden wekt,
Dagen en Daden, en onvergankelijk elk;
Kom tot het Eeuwige, wonend in ons en u,
En dat – als een twijg in verzadigde vloeistof 't zout
Aan en rondom zich kristalliseren doet –
Zo in de Wording van 't Al de tijdlijke woeling
Schept tot kristallen die duren en dus bij mij
De Kristaltwijg heet.

23 November 1902

De Noordzee

De Noordzee doet zijn gore golven dreunen
En laat ze op 't strand in lange lijnen breken.
Zijn voorjaarswater marmren groene streken
En schuim en zwart waaronder schelpen kreunen.

Zie van 't balkon mij naar den einder leunen
Met ogen die sints lang zo wijd niet keken:
Een droom in 't hart is me eer ik 't wist ontweken
En 't oog wil buiten me op iets komends steunen.

But now I returned
To myself and found the youth
Who walked by the town-canals,
And now to that youth
I said this word: yea, truly
Your shyness grew too greatly in you.

For those you love, those who cause your shyness,
Thing and person, person and thing,
They are eternal.
And the love that is within you
And causes you to be shy,
It is eternal.
But you alone have not seen it.

You loved in things, you loved in people
The non-Eternal.
Therein is conflict and the hate that makes power-less,
Therein is death.
But now come to the Eternal that brings forth deeds,
Days and Deeds, imperishable each;
Come to the Eternal dwelling in us and you
And which – as a twig in a saturated fluid
Will make the salt crystallize on and round it –
Makes the short-lived turbulence in the Universe as it grows
Become enduring crystals, and hence its name for me
Is The Crystal Twig.

The North Sea

The North Sea rolls his murky billows booming
And breaking on the shore in stretching lines.
His spring-time water's streaked with marbled greens
And foam and black; below the shells are groaning.

Here on my balcony towards the horizon leaning
I gaze with eyes once more to vastness drawn;
A heart-felt dream before I knew has flown;
My eyes are seeking help from elsewhere coming.

Hoe ben ik altijd weer vervuld, verlaten:
Vervuld van liefde en hoop en schoon geloven;
Verlaten als mijn dromen mij begeven.

Maar dan komt, o Natuur, langs alle straten
Uw kracht, uw groei, uw dreiging, uw beloven –
Hoe klopt mijn hart van nieuw, van eeuwig leven.

20 April 1903

Dichters nachtgezang

6

Liefde is meer dan alle dingen
Die in 't daglicht lokkend staan,
Liefde is dan de erinneringen
Meer die schoonst in schemer gaan,
Liefde is meer dan alle wezens
Die begeren veel en lang
Dat na min of meer belezens
De ene gaat des andren gang,
Liefde is meer dan al 't geziene
Dat door werelds weefstoel drijft,
Nu een warling van 't misschiene
Dan figuur die feilloos blijft, –
Liefde is dat, beweegloos schijnend,
Doet bewegen al wat is,
Nooit verschijnend, nooit verdwijnend,
Helderste en geheimenis, –
Liefde is dat in alle dingen
Leeft en weeft zodat ze zijn,
Liefde is in de erinneringen
De onveranderlijke lijn, –
Liefde is wat in alle wezens
't Hart doet gaan naar andren heen
Zodat zonder iet belezens

How I am evermore fulfilled, forsaken:
Fulfilled with love and hope and beauteous faith;
Forsaken when my very dreams desert me.

But then, o Nature, along all your ways,
Your strength, your growth, your threat come,
    your foretoken –
How my heart beats with life renewed, eternal.

Poet's night hymn

6

Love is more than all appearance
That by day alluring shows,
Love is more than the remembrance
That most fair in twilight grows,
Love is more than all the beings
Who desire so long and pray
That with less or more persuading
One may go the other's way,
Love is more than through the weaving
World-loom unremitting glides,
Chance events now, swiftly fleeting,
Then a form that fast abides, –
Love is that which, moveless seeming,
Lives and moves in all we see,
Never showing, never going,
Radiance and mystery, –
Love is what in all appearance
Lives and weaves so that it is,
Love - in every remembrance
The unchanging steadfastness, –
Love is what in every being
Makes the heart to others turn,
So, without the least persuading

De ene d'aêr zoekt, de ander de een, –
Liefde is wat in al 't geziene
De ene drift is waar 't door drijft,
Liefde is achter al 't misschiene
De een figuur die feilloos blijft.

14 February 1905

Pasen

Op Goede Vrijdag
Is Hij begraven,
Niet in een graf – zijn graf was het hellevuur –,
Doch Zondagmorgen
Was Hij weer opgestaan,
Ging door de velden,
Glimlachend vredig
Naar den hemel van blinkend blauw.

De bloemen stonden,
Trossen en kelken,
Schomlend en wieglend,
Pralend en teder,
Terwijl Hij, kijkend, kwam;
De duinrand waasde,
Leeuwriken schoten –
Paarlen van klank en
Veedren van vreugde –
Door de zonnestralen
Boven Zijn hoofd.

Hij wist niet beter
Of deze dag was
Voor Hem geschapen,
Een dag van de aarde,
Maar zó geheven
Boven het aardgedoe,
Dat alle wandlaars

Each will seek the other one, –
Love is what in all we're seeing
Is the urge that drives and guides,
Love is beyond all that's fleeting
The one form that fast abides.

Easter

On Good Friday
– He was buried,
Not in a grave – his grave was the fire of hell –,
But on Sunday morning
He had arisen,
Went through the fields,
Smiling serenely
To the heaven of limpid blue.

The flowers stood, their
Bells and clusters
Dangling and swaying,
Flaming and tender,
While He, gazing, came;
The dune-ridge was hazy,
Skylarks were darting –
Pearls of sound and
Feathers of gladness –
Amid the sunrays
Over His head.

He could not but feel
This day for Him
Had been created:
A day of the earth,
But so uplifted
Above earth's bustle,
That all the walkers

En lange slierten
Van wielen berijdende
Knapen in gele
Kurassen van de trompetbloem
Hem schenen gezien als uit hogen hemel,
Klein en ver door de slingrende wegen
Van 't landschap, – boden
Van de éne tijding:
'Hij was begraven,
Zijn graf was het hellevuur,
Maar nu is Hij opgestaan,
Ging door de velden,
Steeg op naar den hemel:
Zie hoe Hij neerziet
Op ons en lacht.'

En 's avonds daalde
Hij op Zijn duintop
En zag de velden
Veelkleurig scheemren –
Nog teder blinken –
Zag hoe de zon zich
Baadde in de golven,
Zag hoe de zee zich
Wond om Zijn aarde,
En al de sterren
Stegen en daalden
Rondom Zijn hoofd.

16 September 1906

And trailing streams
Of cyclists, pedalling
Youths in yellow
Cuirasses of trumpet-flowers
Were seen by Him as from highest heaven,
Little and far on the winding roads of
The landscape, – bringers
Of onc glad tidings:
'He had been buried,
His grave was the fire of hell,
But now He has risen,
Went through the fields,
Ascended to Heaven:
See how he gazes
On us and smiles.'

And at eve He descended
On His dune-top
And saw the fields
Many-hued in twilight –
Still gleaming softly –
Saw how the sun then
Bathed in the waves,
Saw the sea
Encircling His earth,
And all the stars that
Rose and descended
Around his head.

In den spiegel van dood en leven

De terrassen van Meudon

De lucht is stil: op eindloos verre heuvlen
Strekt zich de stad in blond en rozig licht –
Ik wend mij om waar lachen klinkt en keuvlen:
Daar kust een knaap een blank en zoet gezicht.

Ik zie omlaag: in vaste en strenge perken
Sombert rondom een kom een herfstge tuin.
Ik zie omhoog: een koepel, zwaar van zerken,
Stijgt, sterrenwacht, hoog boven bomenkruin.

Op trapgesteenten, broklig, maar gebleven,
Blijf ik dan peinzend en in weemoed staan, –
Want dode dingen zijn die langer leven
Dan wij die werden, welken en vergaan.

12 November 1906

Emmausganger

In de gestalte zien wat andren dromen,
Wat voor de meesten vaag verlangen blijft,
Dat was uw voorrecht, Vriend. Een nevel drijft
Dan voor uw oog en 't beeld is weggenomen.

Maar eeuwig zweeft voortaan die vorm u voor:
Gij beeldt hem in uw boek voor laatre geesten,
Gij meet naar hem menslijke smarten, feesten....
Uw heden leent licht van zijn toekomst-gloor.

Gij weet dat nooit, nooit zielen zijn gescheiden
Die elkaar vonden in hun hoogsten bond:
Hun woord klinkt saam: hun kus hoort beider mond,
Hun wens was: vinden, en hun vondst: verbeiden.

In the mirror of death and life

The terraces at Meudon

The air is still: on hills in endless distance
Stretches the town in blond and rosy haze –
I turn to where soft laughter sounds and whispers:
A youth has kissed a sweetly radiant face.

I look below: stern lies there, firmly bounded,
Sombre around a pond an autumn park.
I look on high: a dome, of greystone rounded,
Towers over trees, – built to observe the stars.

On terrace-steps, now crumbling, but enduring,
Pausing in thoughtful wistfulness I stay, –
For lifeless things yet are the longer-during
Than we who, growing, wilting, pass away.

Pilgrim to Emmaus

To see as form what others dream, as visage
The vision for which many vaguely yearn,
That was your fortune, Friend. Then mist was borne
Before your eyes, and you had lost the image.

But evermore that image haunts your view:
You mould it in your book for later morrows,
You measure by it human joys and sorrows....
Your day is lent light by its dawning glow.

You know that for those souls there's no dividing
Who found each other in their sacred troth:
Their word is joint; their kiss for either's mouth:
Their wish was: finding, and their find: abiding.

Zij leven saam: zij leven voor de schaar
Die altijd vraagt en nimmermeer kan vinden.
Zij vindt voortaan in wie elkaar beminden
Haar eigen liefde aanschouwlijk, waar en klaar.

10 January 1907

Aan 't venster

Hul me in fluweel en goud: geef mij mijn vedel.
Open het raam: wat blinkt het landschap blauw!
Flonkre in 't kristal de wijn door bladerschauw!
Strijke mijn hand de snaar verheugd en edel!

Ontsluit dat kistje: zegel, munt en cedel
Is 't kunstrijk gearbeid klein gevang te nauw.
Plaats naast ze – omvangensgraag mijn hand trilt flauw –
D'oogholligen, kaakgrijnzenden, dien schedel.

Zijn ronde bol is de aarde in vasten dood.
Hoe vonkt en straalt en stroomt en ruist zij buiten!
Ik wil die beide in énen blik omsluiten,
Proeven, o aarde, uw schoon dat bleef en vlood.

Nu is uw kleur, verhelderend, valend; – fluiten
Zo zoet, zo teer, als nimmer vogel floot.

22 February 1907

De spiegel

Ik heb mijn spiegel stil omhoog gehouden
En wie gij zaagt was waarlijk wel uzelf.
Zie maar uw ogen die mijn glas mistrouwden!

They live together, live forever here
For those who, always seeking, never find.
They'll find from now in these whose hearts were joined
Their own love truly imaged, sheer and clear.

At the window

Deck me in velvet, gold: hand me my viol.
Open the window: how the land gleams blue!
Let wine-filled glass sparkle in foliage-shadow!
Sound now, my hand, the strings sublime and joyful!

Open that casket: seal and coin and scroll
Are too hemmed in by their wrought prison now.
Place by them – keen to grasp I tremble to –
That hollow-eyed, jaw-grinning one, the skull.

Its rounded dome is Earth when rigid, dead.
Outside it's glittering, shining, streaming, purling!
I will see both in one regard encircling,
Tasting thy beauty, Earth, that's stayed and fled.

Thy hue, grown clear, is fading now; – there's piping
So sweet, so rare, as never piped a bird.

The mirror

I held my mirror steadily uplifted:
The one you saw was verily yourself.
Just see your eyes in glass which they mistrusted!

Ik die uit licht strenge gestalten delf
Alleen door 't heffen van mijn blanken spegel,
Kon dat niet doen als niet uw wezenswelf

Zich indrukte in mijn schijn gelijk een zegel.
Gij zijt daar wel, maar vindt u toch niet gans?
Gij speurt vergeefs naar wat geheimen regel

Mijn glas u kaatste en uitwiste in zijn glans,
Zodat ge er zijt en niet zijt, blijde en boze
Al naar ge 't merkt? Luister, ik zeg het thans:

Het toont u 't wezen, wiste 't wezen-loze.

1 March 1907

Cirkelloop

Ik ben een vonk die doelloos, richtingloos,
Geworpen in 't heelal mijn vaart begon,
Toen bond me aldra aan zich een andre zon
En wentlend leef ik ongemeten poos,

Een kern van leven, in zichzelven voos,
Vol van de kracht die in en rond mij spon.
O dat ik zonder weten eeuwig kon
Wentlen in de onbegrepen stralenroos.

Oneindge wereld, onvoltooid heelal
En onbegonnen, maar waarin elk deel
Beeld van het heel is en een lichtgespeel

Langs de eeuwge banen, zeg, zal eenmaal, zal
Ooit zijn het eind van uw gestaadgen brand,
Gij diamant in 't holle van een hand?

23 October 1907

Although from light stern forms I delve
By merely raising my bright mirror, still
I could not do so if your being's curve

Weren't in my gleam imprinted like a seal.
You're there indeed, yet find not every line?
You vainly search by what mysterious rule

My glass reflects and melts you in its sheen,
So that you're there and not there, pleased, resentful
Accordingly? Listen, I'll say it then:

It shows you essence, melts the inessential.

Orbit

I am a spark that, trendless, purposeless,
Thrown in the universe began my run;
Soon I was drawn then by another sun,
And turning live a while yet measure-less,

A core of life, itself devoid of stress,
Full of the force that in and round me spun.
O that aloft, unknowing I could turn
Eternally in the strange sphere of rays.

Unending world, unconsummated All
And unbegun, but wherein every part
Is likeness of the whole and play of light

Along the eternal ways – shall one day, shall
Ever thy fire perpetual come to end,
Thou diamond in the hollow of a hand?

Ares en Afrodite

Mij roept geen vrouw of ik herken den klank.
Háár zag ik drijvende gelijk een lijk
Onder mij door de ruimte, blond en rijk
Het hangend haar, het golvend lichaam blank.

En een geluid toog als een zilvren rank
Over het uitspansel en eer ik wijk
Voelde ik over mijn rug een zacht gestrijk
Van net dat bond me. Ik viel gelijk een plank.

Door zeven heemlen viel ik. Ik herken
Het lachen van de goden daar ik rust
Op haar: zij lachte en hield mijn mond gekust.

En heel de hemel herbegon zijn loop.
Ik lag in schaamte en wond me uit zilvren knoop.
Ik hoor den klank en voel weer wie ik ben.

October 1907

Het spiegelbeeld

Ik wendde me om als om mijzelf te zien.
De spiegel kaatste me in een ander glas:
Ik zag het stil en wist dat ik die was
En op mijn lippen beeft een vaag 'misschien'....

Ik zag mijzelf: ik mag aan andre liën
Niet tonen wat ik weet: ik treed een pas
Terzijde en wend mij dan een oogwenk ras
Terug. Wee mij! wat baat het nu te vliën.

Want opgericht als aanstonds sta ik daar.
De spiegel houdt op donkren grond mijn beeld.
Kome wie komt: het staat daar angstig-klaar.

Ares and Aphrodite

No woman calls me but I hear that sound.
Her I saw floating – a drowned form she seemed –
There under me through space, lovely and blond
Her hanging hair, her surging body gleamed.

And a thin twang like silver strands I heard
Across the firmament, and ere I broke
Away, I just felt something gently stroke
My back – a net closed. I fell like a board.

Through seven heavens I fell. Into my mind
Comes the gods' roaring laughter, as I rest
On her: she laughed and held my mouth tight-kissed.

And all the heavens' spheres resumed their course.
I lay in shame and stripped the silver noose.
Hearing the sound, once more myself I find.

The mirror image

I had turned round as though myself to see.
The mirror cast me on another glass.
I saw it, stunned, and knew that such I was,
And on my lips trembles a vague 'maybe'....

I saw myself, and I must not betray
To others what I know: I step a pace
Aside, and then again one moment face
The glass. Woe's me! it's useless now to flee.

Because full-length as then I'm standing there.
The mirror holds me on dark ground portrayed.
Whoever comes: I stand there ghastly clear.

Is dit uw glas, dat mij mijzelf ontsteelt,
En gij onthult mij nooit dit groot gevaar,
Duldt dat ik, kind, heb met uw gaaf gespeeld?

October 1907

Het aarde-lief

Gij vraagt mij of ik niet een ander liefheb,
Of niet uw liefde me enkel dient opdat
Ik schoon ervan verhaal aan 't hoogre Lief.
Ik antwoord: neen. Ik heb uw stil gedrag,
Uw woorden en den eenvoud van uw wezen,
Zó lief, dat ik er gans in wil vergaan.
En 'k zeg u meer: uw onschuld is zo groot,
Dat als die Andre komt en ik mij buig,
Gij in 't verheven aanschijn niet zult zien –
Wat ik toch weet en wat ik nooit vergeet –
Dat wat daar ziel aan geeft, is uw gelaat.

Spring 1908

De zangstem

Niemand weet hoezeer
Ik naar u verlang,
Zoetste en laatste zang,
Slaap en dan niet meer.

Zoetste en laatste zang
Die zich traag bevrij'.
Dan – alsof ik vlij
Wang aan zachte wang.

Is this *thy* glass, which makes me my own shade,
And thou hast never laid this danger bare,
Brookst that I, child, with thy dread gift have played?

The earthly beloved

You ask me if I do not love another,
If not your love will merely help me tell
Its tale of beauty to the higher Love.
I answer: no. I love your quiet bearing,
Your speaking and your still integrity
So deeply – I would wholly merge therein.
And I'll say more: your innocence is such,
That, when the Other comes and I bow down,
You will not see in the high countenance –
What yet I know and never can forget –
The living soul then given is your face.

The singing voice

None can ever know
How for you I long,
Last and sweetest song,
Sleep and then no more.

Last and sweetest song,
Slowly drifting through…
Then – as though I drew
Cheek soft cheek along.

Wang aan wang ik vlij,
Maar de zangtoon drijft
Donker door, en blijft
Tot aan de overzij.

Zelfde zangtoon blijft
Bij me aan de overkant.
Zelfde die mijn hand·
Hier in woorden schrijft.

Zelfde die mijn hand
Hier verwoordt, is daar
Woordeloos en klaar:
Vlam die zingend brandt.

Woordeloos en klaar
Eent zich daar de toon
Met den droom van schoon
Die maar hoopt op haar.

Uit mijn droom van schoon
Wens ik telkens weer
Dat de zangstem keer',
Dat zij in mij woon'.

O zo ze eens niet keer'?
Vrezend roep ik bang:
Zoetste en laatste zang,
Slaap en dan niet meer.

21–22 February 1911

Cheek by cheek I draw,
But the singing glides
Darkly on, and bides
Till on yonder shore.

Still the singing bides
With me in that land,
Singing, which my hand
Here in words now writes.

What my hand portrays
Here in words, now there
Wordless glows and clear;
Burns – a singing blaze.

Wordless does the clear
Strain there merge its tone
With the dream which fain
Still that song would hear.

From my dream I fain
Would now that the pure
Song might come once more,
That it were my own.

O, may it come no more?
I call, by fear unstrung:
Last and sweetest song,
Sleep and then no more.

De uitredding

Zult gij niet altijd komen
Als ik u minst verwacht?
Beminde van mijn dromen,
Zon in mijn nacht!

Ik heb mij neergeworpen
In slijk op 't lichtloos pad,
Bloedge vampyren slorpen
Zich aan mij zat.

Mijn mond vol bittre vruchten,
Mijn hart leeg als een hel,
De lucht zwaar van de zuchten
Die 'k niet meer tel.

Tot, zie, een schijn zich kondigt,
Spokig geheester door
Dat als een ziel die zondigt
Zijn loof verloor.

Een schijn, zie, door die naaktheid
Snelt snel nabij me en slaat
– O schaam-doende geraaktheid –
Mij in 't gelaat.

Waar red, waar berg ik 't aanschijn,
Graaf me in den morsgen grond!
Droeg ooit een mens zijn aanzijn
In 't licht, zó wond?

Maar als met handen neemt gij
Mijn hand van voor mijn oog,
Als met uw adem zeemt gij
Mijn wangen droog.

En als een kind geheven
Op armen, zie ik nu
Alleen uw ogen leven,
Uw lippen, u!

24 September 1911

The deliverance

Won't you be always coming
When least I think to wait?
Beloved of my dreaming,
Sun in my night!

I've hurled myself and tumbled
On murky paths in mud,
Gluttonous vampires guzzle,
Drunk, on my blood.

My mouth with wry fruit bitter,
My heart empty like hell,
My breath with panting tighter
Than tongue can tell.

Till, see, a glimmer's dawning
Through ghostlike brushwood yews
Which like a soul that's sinning
Bear naked boughs.

And then – see – through that bareness
Swiftly a flash of light
Strikes me with shaming brightness
Blinding my sight.

Where save, where hide my features,
Dig myself in foul moor!
Did ever human creature
Face light, só sore?

But as with hands you're leading
My hand from off my eye,
As with your mouth you're breathing
My sad cheeks dry.

And like a child you're lifting
In arms, so now I do
See your sole eyes, the living,
Your warm lips, you!

Verschijning

Hunkren doe ik vaak nog naar uw adem,
Naar uw ogen, naar uw donkre haren,
En ik schrei en zucht omdat uw liefde
Nooit mij meer verstaan zal en verwarmen.

Maar dan komt gij met uw rijkste glimlach
Vóór mij staan en zegt: "mijn lieve meester,
Was uw leven niet altijd het mijne,
En het mijne 't uwe, zodat beide

Onafscheidlijk samen zijn gestorven,
Onafscheidlijk samen zijn gebleven
In de erinring die gij nu moet dragen?
Ik die nu hier sta in uw erinring

Blijf met u, al moet gij nog verandren,
En wat mijn was blijft met mij hetzelfde,
Gij ook, en geen wissling kan u deren,
Schoon gij groeit in mij weer vreemde tijden.

Want wel is terugkeer niemand mooglijk,
Maar wat was blijft in hem tegenwoordig,
En ik ben voortaan die u de vrede
Van dat ongerept bestaan verzeker."

Dan verdwijnt gij als een mens in nevel,
En ik voel uw zoete stem mij strelen,
En ik proef de geur nog van uw haren,
En uw armen voel ik mij omarmen.

1 January 1913

Note. This poem was addressed to the memory of Alex Gutteling,
the poet loved by Verwey as his spiritual son who died young
(1884–1910).

Apparition

Yearning do I still feel for your breath,
For your eyes and for your dark-brown hair,
And I weep and sigh as your affection
Nevermore will understand and warm me.

Then you come, and generously smiling
Stand before me saying: "my dear master,
Was not always your life one with mine,
As my life was yours, so that the two

Have now died inseparable together,
And inseparable together stayed
In remembrance which you now must bear?
I who now here stand in your remembrance

Stay with you, though you must go on changing,
And what was mine, stays with me unchanging,
You along with it; no change can harm you,
Though you'll grow in times I shall not know of.

For indeed return is possible to no-one,
But the past within him remains present,
And henceforth I'm he through whom the peace
Stays intact of your bygone existence."

Then you fade as though in misty weather,
And I'm feeling how your sweet voice soothes me,
Sensing still the fragrance of your hair,
Round me still your arms as they embrace me.

Oneindigheid

Van honderdduizend jaren her
Kwam tot mijn oog de straal van een ster,
Hij kuste mij met zijn milde licht,
Ik voelde mij leven als in een gedicht,
Want wat is tijd?

Meer mijlen ver dan mens verstaat
Bewoog mijn oog dat stergelaat,
Ik was nabij haar met mijn blik
En ondervond een zoeten schrik:
Geen ruimte telt!

Tezaam geschapen ster en oog,
Eén enkel leven laag en hoog,
Zijn wij de gewordenen voor elkaar,
Zij werd door mij, ik werd voor haar:
Waar is de grens?

Ik draag en ben het heel heelal.
O valse schijn van lichaamswal,
Waarbinnen wij schijnen, waarbuiten wij zijn,
Omvangende in een gedroomde lijn
De oneindigheid!

17–18 February 1913

Hapering

Als ik denk dat ik van u moet scheiden,
Aarde en zon en heel dit lieve leven,
Stil staat dan mijn hart, al duurt het even....
Als ik denk dat ik van u moet scheiden.
Dwaas, bezweer ik dan de vlugge tijden
Stilstand: die niet anders is dan sneven –
Als ik denk dat ik van u moet scheiden,
Aarde en zon en heel dit lieve leven.

Infinity

From countless scores of light-years far
Came to my eye the ray of a star;
It kissed me with its mellow light,
I saw my life with a poet's sight,
For what is time?

More miles away than man can trace
My eye was moved by that star's face;
I was near-by her with my gaze
And underwent a sweet amaze:
No space does count!

Created jointly, star and eye,
– One single life, below, on high –
We grew to be each other's pair,
She grew through me, I grew for her:
Where are the bounds?

I bear and am the universe.
O falsely seeming bodily bars!
We are beyond what seems to confine,
Embracing in an imagined line
Infinity!

Halting

When I think that I shall have to leave you,
Earth and sun and all this life so lovely,
Still then stands my heart, if for one moment....
When I think that I shall have to leave you.
Foolish then, I would adjure Time's fleeting
Stillness: which is nothing if not dying –
When I think that I shall have to leave you,
Earth and sun and all this life so lovely.

Vizioen op Boschwijk

Binnen de donkre cirkelmuur,
Met riet gedekt,
Van voren open naar het uitzicht toe
Van weiden onder 't zwaar gebladert door
Van weerzijds linde en eik,
Zit hij en leest.
Erachter is de kom,
De zwarte vijver,
Waarrondom linden staan.
De grijze dag is over 't weiland zilver,
De leeuwrik rijst, de koeien grazen,
De verre horizon leeft roerloos-rijk, –
Hij leest en schrijft.
De blaadren achter hem zijn vol gesuis,
Het water vloeit onhoorbaar saam,
De donkre schaduwen zijn vormloos stil, –
Hij zit in schaduw en hij schrijft en peinst.
En stilte en verte en scheemring en geluid
Vloeien ineen tot woorden....
Hij peinst en schreit.

5 June 1913

Droomtij

Hoe is de hemel zo nabij!
Ben ik in hem of hij in mij?

Laat los! Mijn vaartuig, nu voor stroom,
Voelt zich getrokken naar de Droom.

Gij spreekt tot mij, gij ziet mij aan –
Ik zie u in de verte staan.

Ik leef al in een ander land –
Van d'oever wuift voor 't laatst uw hand.

9 March 1915

Vision at Boschwijk★

Within the dark encircling wall
Covered with thatch, –
In front it opens towards the distant view
Of meadows showing under heavy foliage
Of flanking lime and oak, –
He sits and reads.
Behind him is the pool,
The sombre pond,
Around which lime-trees stand.
The grey day hovers over meadows: silver,
The skylark rises, cows are grazing,
The far horizon lives and, moveless, shines –
He reads and writes.
The leaves behind him stir with mellow murmur,
The water flows and joins inaudibly,
The shadows, dark, are formless, and lie still, –
He sits in shadow and he writes and dreams.
And stillness, distance, twilight and the sounds
Flow and merge in words....
He dreams and weeps.

★Boschwijk was the country seat of the pre-Romantic poet Rhynvis Feith (1753–1824), the first among Dutch poets to cultivate melancholy sentiment and exalted love, seen against a background of beautiful, preferably autumnal landscapes.

Dream-tide

How is it, heaven's so near-by!
Can I be there, is heaven in me?

Let go! My vessel, now mid-stream,
Feels gently drawn towards the Dream.

You speak to me, look in my eye –
I see you standing far away.

I've moved into another land –
From yonder once more waves your hand.

Sterven

Zwijg maar. Ik weet. Ik beluister altijd uw gedachten.
Waren het koekoeken die in het griendhout lachten?
Was het de blikkring van zon op de stroom die mijn zinnen
Plotsling verwarde? Of schoot me een vertelsel te binnen
Van een fluitspelende knaap die de landen doorreisde,

Tot hij, staande onder een galg, op eenmaal vergrijsde,

Voelend de strop om zijn hals en de zonnevonken
Ziende op het water? De rode dorpsdaken blonken,
Zang kwam van volk uit de verte, en geklop van werven.

Blauw was de hemel en straalde, en hij moest sterven.
Zwijg maar. Ik weet: wij bezitten niets dan dit éne.
Wie heeft het leven niet lief! En ge wenst dat ik wene?
Niet zo dwaas! Omdat ik mijn ziel heb verloren
Juist aan dat ene, kan ik niet anders dan horen
Naar het inwendig gezang van ons tweeër vreugde.
Dronken ben ik, als een die wijnen teugde.
En – wij bezitten elkander. Wat zou de wereld
Zijn zo ze niet door mijn ooglicht werd overpereld.
Al ons tezamen beleven is in ons getekend.
Zal het ooit einden? Een dwaas die bij uren rekent.
Nochtans –luister!– wij hebben een donker vermoeden
Dat wij bijeen behóren: als wilgeroeden
Wuivend in blauwe lucht, omlaag verbonden.
't Oppervlaksspel van ons leven heeft wislijk gronden.
   Ik duik omlaag, lief, of ik u verlaat:
   In heldere afgrond groet mij uw gelaat.

Undated

Note. This poem was addressed to Kitty van Vloten, Verwey's wife.

Dying

Speak not. I know. I always follow your thinking.
Was it those cuckoos that laughed in the osier-thicket?
Was it the glitter of sunlight on water that suddenly stirred
My senses? Or did I remember that story I heard
Of a young flute-player who through many countries had
    travelled,
Till, standing under a gallows, he suddenly aged and
    shrivelled,
Feeling the noose round his neck as he saw the sun-sparks
Flickering on the water? The red village-roofs glowed,
Singing came from afar, of workmen, hammering from the
    quayside.
Blue was the sky and radiant – and he was to die.
Speak not. I know: there is nothing but this we have.
Who is there that loves not life? and you'd wish me to weep?
Not so foolish! Because it is to that only my soul is given
Wholly and utterly, I cannot do other than listen
To the inner hymn that sings our united joy.
Drunken I am, like one who has drunk deeply of wine.
And – we have each other. What were the world,
If it were not by the light of my eyes overpearl'd?
All our life together is engraved in our hearts.
Will it ever end? A fool that would reckon by hours.
And yet –listen!– we have got a dark awareness
That we *belong* together: like twigs of willows
Swaying in the blue sky, yet jointly grounded.
Surely the surface-play of our lives is deeply founded.
    I dive down, love, and seem to go my ways:
    In the clear deep I'm greeted by your face.

Meidag

Hoe nabij,
Hoe als eerst,
Glanst het bosje en straalt de wei,
Schalt de leeuwrik die met zang de lucht beheerst.

Zorgenvol
Liep ik uit,
Eer ik 't wist kwam Lente en zwol
De ogen vol met groen me, de oren vol geluid.

Wie bleef jong?
Wie werd oud?
Lente lachte en *mijn* hart zong
De eigen tonen over die ze een knaap vertrouwt.

May 1917

De spiegel zelf

Gij nadert mij en spiegelt u
En dacht ge waart een kind van nu,
Maar ziet uzelf als eeuwigheid,
Als naakt en rein en vrij van tijd.

Gij schreit en wilt niet dat dit beeld
Dat uw toevallige schoonheid heelt
En niets is dan uw blijvende aard
Door mij als 't uwe wordt bewaard.

En zegt: is niet een spiegeling
In waarheid een verganklijk ding?
En zó verganklijk ben ik ook:
Een bloem die even openlook.

May Day

How near by,
How like then,
Gleams the copse and shines the fen,
Rings the skylark that with song commands the sky.

Full of cares
Forth I went,
Ere I knew came Spring and sent
My eyes agaze with greenery, full of sound my ears.

Who stayed young?
Who grew old?
Spring came, smiled – and *my* heart sang
Anew the very tones she will to a youth unfold.

The mirror speaks

You face me, and I mirror you,
Who thought yourself a child of now,
But see your own eternity,
Naked and pure, from time set free.

You weep and will not let this form,
Which veils your evanescent charm
But is your soul's enduring shape,
Stay as your own, for me to keep,

And say: is not a mirroring
In very truth a fleeting thing?
And fleeting, too, is what I am:
A flower just opening into bloom.

Waarom dan laat gij me enkel zien
Wat ik niet ben, wat ik misschien
Wanneer ik dood ben eens zal zijn:
Een onvergankelijke schijn?

En ik: gij hebt wel nooit bedacht
Dat niemand met meer recht die klacht
Zou kunnen slaken dan ikzelf.
Ik zoek u vrouw, ik vind u elf.

Ik ben geboren met die ban
Waarbuiten ik niet treden kan.
Ik smacht naar menselijke min
En zie alleen de mythe erin.

De mythe is in me als breukloos glas:
Zij spiegelt zich in al wat was,
In al wat is en toont elkeen
Het beeld aan hem en haar gemeen.

Zij maakt de tuin tot paradijs,
De wereld tot een vreemde wijs
Waarvan het hart de zin verstaat,
En toont in mensen 't godsgelaat.

En al wat toeval heet, valt af,
Als duivel of als aas voor 't graf,
Waarheen zij schouwt; maar iedre groei
Straalt voor haar oog in duurbre bloei.

Zij is mijn Lente: ik heb om haar
Wreed getrotseerd herhaald gevaar
Van mijn lichamelijke dood,
Tot zij mij heel in de armen sloot

En sprak: zie nu, geen schepsel leeft
Waarnaar uw hart niet smacht en beeft,
Maar allen hebben iets van mij,
Dat en niet anders, neem ook gij,

Why do you only let me see
What I am not, what will maybe
When I am dead of me remain:
A likeness then for ever mine?

And I: you surely never thought
That no one with more justice could
Deplore this feature than myself.
I seek you woman, find you elf.

I have been born within this ban
Too stern to break – I never can.
I yearn for simple human love,
Seeing love's myth is all I prove.

Myth is within me, flawless glass,
The mirror held to all that was
To all that is; and each is shown
The image shared with her alone.

She makes the garden paradise,
The world a singing strange and wise
Of which the heart will feel the sense,
And shows in men God's countenance.

And all that's chance will drop away,
To death or devil fall a prey,
Which she beholds; but all that grows
Before her eye with blossom glows.

She is my Spring: I have for her
Sternly braved dangers that recur
Of bodily death in many forms,
Till she enclosed me in her arms

And spoke: see, there's no soul that lives
Whom thy heart yearns not for and loves,
But all have something that is mine:
That, and nought else, be also thine,

Zodat wie meest van mij bezit,
Meest u behoort. Alleen nog dit:
Geen enkle mens hoort andren heel:
Elk heeft aan de andre als aan mij deel.

Zo zij. En nu staat midden-in
Mijn hart die Lente, en ik begin
De wereld als een deel van haar
Te zien, zo naakt, zo schuldloos klaar.

En gij staat voor me en wilt er zijn
Nog bloeiender dan dit festijn
Van onvergankelijke vreugd
Dat u omarmt. Een eeuwge jeugd,

Schoner dan uw kortstondige praal,
Schijnt door uw wezen, zendt een straal
Van blijdschap door uw ogen uit,
Uw leden zijn een golf, die sluit

En opent de geheimenis:
Begeerte die een geven is,
En als een kussen, nu 't heelal
Beweegt onder uw harenval,

Zijn landen en de grote zee,
Alsof er lokkende vergleê
Een meermin naar het flonkrend diep –
Hoor hoe zij riep, u riep, mij riep....

Maar zie, de zee is klaar, de plek
In 't bosje is als een feestvertrek,
En op een omgeworpen stam
Gaan onze woorden als een vlam

Die heen- en weertongt door het groen.
Het schoppen van uw kleine schoen
Ontrust een hagedis: die schiet
Langs 't kleurge mos naar 't donkre riet.

So those who most of me possess
Shall most be thine. But think of this:
None wholly can belong to thee:
Each only shares what is of me.

Thus she. And now there stands within
My heart that Spring, and I begin
To see the world as part of her,
So naked, innocent and clear.

And you before me want to be
More blooming than this ecstasy
Of sheer imperishable joy
Embracing you. Eternal youth,

Lovelier than your short-lived grace,
Shines through your being, sending rays
Of gladness from your smiling eyes;
Your limbs are like a wave that hides

And yet reveals the mystery:
Desire that is a giving free
And is like kissing, as the whole
World moves beneath your full hair's fall

Its lands, and moves the mighty sea
As if a mermaid's luring shape
Were gliding towards the sparkling deep –
Hear how she called, called you, called me....

But look, the sea is clear, the dune-
Spinney is like a festive room
And on a trunk that's fallen down
Our words go tonguing like a flame

Through the green shadow to and fro.
The kicking of your little shoe
Disturbs a lizard, and it speeds
Along gay moss to darker reeds.

Waarom is nu het duin zo hoog?
Wat maakt de zee een grote boog
Van onafzienbre horizon!
En als een koning straalt de zon.

Ik weet niet wat ge nog begeert.
Mijn rijk is 't uwe. Zeewind keert
Zijn zilte lippen naar uw mond.
Wij staan zo menselijk gezond

En vol in 't leven: heel niet als
Gedroomde schimmen die met vals
Gebaar en een verheven schijn
Zich goden huichlen die niet zijn.

Werklijk als wij is wel geeneen.
Zo is mijn Lente. Als heerlijk leen
Gaf zij ons deze onsterflijkheid,
Dit ogenblik, deze eeuwigheid.

Spring 1917

Zielsdrang

De late lente bracht de bloei
Van vroege bloemen, trage bomen
Opeens tezaam tot zulk een dag
Als schaars voordien de wereld zag,
En geuren die door lovers stromen
Vervingen wind die zuidwaarts woei.

Hoe heb ik vroeger niet geschreid
Als ik de voorjaars-fee ontmoette.
Haar jonkheid en verganklijkheid
Bewogen 't woord waar ik mee groette.
Maar toch rees in mijn hart de kreet:
Hoè broos en teer, gij kunt niet sterven:

Why does the dune now rise so high?
How wide the sea along the sky
Draws the immense horizon's line
And how the sun does kingly shine!

I know not why your heart still yearns.
My realm is yours. The sea-wind turns
His salty lips towards your mouth.
We stand here, human, full of health

And strongly living – quite unlike
Dream-begot phantoms who with fake
Gestures and with exalted mien
Would pose as gods who've never been.

Real like us is surely none.
So is my Spring. Her gracious boon
Lent us this immortality,
This moment, this eternity.

Soul urge

Belated spring has brought the blossoms
Of early flowers, tardy trees
Together suddenly – a day
Such as but rarely earth brings forth,
And odours through the foliage flowing
Have ousted tempests from the North.

How I have wept in former days
Encountering the Maid of Spring!
Her youthfulness, her beauty fleeting
Moved me to speak the word of greeting,
Yet in my heart arose the cry:
Frail as you are, you cannot die:

Het is een schijn als wij u derven:
Gij zijt! is 't zeekre dat ik weet.
Nu schreide ik weer, maar om 't erkennen
Dat ze in ons leeft, dat ons geslacht
Van de aanvang haar heeft meegebracht,
Een ziel met toegevouwen pennen,
Maar die zij altijd onverwacht
Weer rept als wij hun vaart ontwennen –
Die zich in blad en bloesem toont
En in de vroege loofgewaden,
In voorjaars hemel en de zaden
Van schepslen waar haar geest in woont,
Doch die 't natuurlijke gebeuren
Niet hoeft, het aanziet als een kleed,
Waarboven zij zich op kan beuren
En dan eerst heel ons eigen heet.

Dan zien we om haar de wereld ronden,
Haar hoogten en haar diepe gronden
Verdwijnen voor de blik die zwijmt,
Maar 't naaste en verste blijft gebonden
Als aan het woord het woord dat rijmt.

De jeugd van alle tijden luistert
Naar tonen die de wijze mond
Van de oudste vinders heeft gefluisterd,
Naar elk lied dat ons niets verkondt
Dan 't bloeien van de hazelaren,
Pronk van kastanjes kandelaren
En zoetheid die de meidoorn zond.

Daarom beginnen de gezichten
En liedren van verrukte vrouwen,–
Of zij verlangen in gedichten
Of zich verzadigen in schouwen,–
Altijd met lente: Pinkstergloeden
Zijn 't vuur waar zij hun hart meê voeden
En dat de wereld over brandt
En dat zij dronken van begeren
Mee willen dragen in de sferen
Van een onsterflijk voorjaarsland.

'Tis a delusion that we lose you:
You are! is what I deeply know.
Once more I've wept, in recognising
That in our heart she lives: mankind
Has harboured her from its arising,
A soul with wings indeed still folded,
Whose sudden beat will overcome us
With mighty and unwonted speed.
In leaves and blossom she appears
And in the early foliage-garments,
In skies of spring and in the offspring
Of beings in whom her spirit dwells –
And yet she needs not nature's cycle,
The garment that's her outward sign,
Which she'll outsoar till she has grown
Into a soul our very own.

The world is seen revolving round her,
Its mountains and its deep ravines
Dissolve before our failing gaze,
But near and far are jointly seen
As word paired with its rhyme-word blends.

The young of all the ages listen
To notes which in their pristine lore
The ancient minstrels' lips did whisper –
Songs that announce us nothing more
Than: see, now bloom the hazel trees!
Soon will the chestnut candles soar
And hawthorn sweetness fill the breeze.

Therefore will always women's visions
And songs of ecstasy begin,–
Whether their yearnings rise to singing
Or they are stilled in contemplation,–
With spring: the fires of Pentecost
Are ever their hearts' nourishment,
A blaze that glows in every land,
Those ardours which, transfixed by yearning
They long to carry with them, turning
Towards an immortal springtime land.

Niets dan de lente en die volkomen!
Dat is de zielsdrang die de dromen
Van alle volken heeft bevuurd
Dat die door de eeuwen hen geleidden,
En alle vormen, alle tijden
Zijn niets dan déze vorm die duurt.

Spring 1917

Als hij niet was

Als hij niet was wien ik gelijk wil zijn
Zou ik niet weten, in mijn pijn,
Waarheen te gaan. Hij is mijn trooster.
Hij maakt mij telkens weer gerust
Als hij de hete kolen blust
Van 't haatvuur op mijn harterooster.

Zijn ogen zijn zo zoet en koel,
Ik staar erin met diep vertrouwen.
Van alle dingen die ik voel
Heeft, zachter dan de blik van vrouwen,
De zijne een reine spiegeling,
Die meer is, want zij is het wezen.
Ik kan er al de waarheid lezen
Waarnaar ik in mij vruchtloos ding.

Hij heeft een woordenloos omarmen
Waarin 'k mij eeuwig veilig weet.
Siddrend en vast is zijn erbarmen
Dat sterkend indringt in mijn leed
Zodat het blijdschap wordt naarbuiten.
Ik ken mijzelf dan niet. Ik ben
Weer licht, maar met een nieuw bekoren.
Kon ik hem heel voor elk ontsluiten,
De wereld werd als nieuw geboren:
Elk had hem lief zoals hij hen.

July 1917

Nothing but spring – a spring consummate!
That is the soul-urge which inspires
All peoples' visions with the fires
By which through time they have been guided,
And all the forms to them betided
Are but this one form – which endures.

If he were not

If he were not, whose like I want to be,
I should not know then, in my pain,
Whither to turn. He's my consoler.
He always stills my aching soul
When he will quench the burning coal
Of hatred's fire in my heart's furnace.

His eyes are always sweet and cool,
I gaze into them deeply trusting.
Of all things that I ever feel
His glance, more than a woman's soothing
Reflects a limpid mirroring
That's more yet, for it is their being.
I find all truth there for my reading
Which I within me seek in vain.

He has a wordless still embracing
Where I'm eternally at peace.
Shuddering and firm is his compassion,
Whose strengthening merges with my grief
Till it grows joyful in appearance.
I know myself not then. I am
So light again, but new-adorned.
If to all men I could reveal him,
The world were as if newly born;
All gave him love as he gives them.

Het lied van de erkentenis

Als ik u kon vinden,
Ingeboren
Tweespraak van mijn ziel, –
Fluistringen omwinden,
Als door voren,
De Verborgene voor wie ik kniel; –
Als ik u kon klaren,
Raadselige tegenstrijdigheid,
Die de mensen honen
Als mijn openbaren
U waagt tonen,
Maar die nochtans de ongeschonden waarheid zijt; –
Al ik u kon grijpen,
Ingeschapen tweestrijd van 't heelal,
Wortel, en u tot een bloem doen rijpen
Aan de telgen van mijn zanggeschal; –
Wie zou dan begeren,
Dronken, in dat bloemgelaat
Zich te spieglen en niet eindlijk leren
Alle schijn die gij niet zijt te ontberen,
Zalig in de erkentnis dat hij u verstaat. –

Geen eigen wil: een droomgelaat,
Geen denkend brein dat wijst en leidt,
Buiten besef van ruimte en tijd
Een mens die innerlijk verstaat

En alles voelt en niets begeert
En wacht het leed dat geen ontgaat:
De nagel die aan 't kruis hem slaat
En de arme mensheid die hem deert.

En ondanks alles, boven al,
De onoverwinbre zaligheid
Die in hem leeft en als hij sterft
Niet voor die andren sterven zal,
Maar blijft als deel dat elk verwerft
Die wordt als hij en met hem lijdt.

The song of recognition

If I could but find you,
Deep-inborn
Converse of my soul, –
Whisperings entwine him,
Furrow-formed,
The Recondite One to whom I kneel; –
If I could illumine
Your mysterious self-conflictingness,
For which men revile you
When I boldly venture
To reveal you,
Though you are indeed inviolate truth; –
If I could but hold you,
Inborn inner conflict of the world,
Root, and like a flower unfold you
On the branches of my song unfurled; –
Who would not be yearning,
Swooning, in that flower-countenance
To be mirrored till the final learning
Came to him who, from appearance turning
Found the still fulfilment of your cognizance. –

No self-will: a dream-countenance,
No thinking brain that leads and guides;
Beyond all sense of space and time
A man of inner cognizance,

Who, feeling all things, nought desires,
Bides inescapable distress:
The nail that clamps him on the cross,
And poor mankind that stirs his tears.

And despite all things, above all,
The bliss invincible, the joy
That lives in him, and at his death
For other people will not die,
But stays, a heritage for all
Who, suffering like him, share his faith.

Nooit kan ik u scheiden,
Levend wezen dat uzelf behoort,
Uit de stroom van dingen en van tijden
Met wie ge eeuwig een zijt als geslacht en soort.

Nochtans, telkens weder,
Uit de schaduw die mijn hart vervult,
Wiekt een Droom, de schitterende veder
In de straling van zijn eigen glans verhuld.

Blijkt ook die verbonden
Aan een afkomst, aan een volk als hij?
Ach, zijn schoonheid bergt zo diepe gronden
Dat geen menslijk oog ze peilt of komt nabij.

Anders gij dan ik.*
Al de inhouden van uw wezen
Anders dan de mijne elk ogenblik.
Anders gij dan ik.

Anders ik dan gij.
Als een vreemde uit altijd vreemder
Wereld groet ik u en kent gij mij.
Anders ik dan gij.

Ware ik u gelijk!
Hoe ge 't wenst, en dringt gedurig
Dat de scheidsmuur tussen ons bezwijk.
Ware ik u gelijk!

Ach, mijn glimlach groeit.
Lief heb ik in u dat andre
Dat me uit al uw daden lokt en boeit.
Ach, mijn glimlach groeit.

*These 48 lines were addressed to Stefan George.

Never can I part you,
Living soul who are your very own,
From the stream of beings and of ages,
With whom you are ever one in race and kind.

– And yet, evermore appearing
From the shade with which my heart is filled
Wings a Dream whose feathers' glittering
By the radiance of its gleam are veiled.

Is it, also, bounded
By a race, a nation where it's born?
Ah, its beauty is so deeply founded
That no human eye can plumb it or discern.

Unlike, you and I.
All the experiences within you
Are at every moment unlike mine.
Unlike, you and I.

Unlike, I and you.
As a stranger from an ever stranger
World I greet you and am known by you.
Unlike, I and you.

Were I but your like!
How you wish it, always urging
That the wall which parts us should now break.
Were I but your like!

Ah, my smile now grows.
For I love in you what's unlike,
What in all your actions charms and draws.
Ah, my smile now grows.

O mijn liefste vriend,
Mij die ge anders wenst omarmend,
Mij die glimlach, vreugdvol op u ziend,
O mijn liefste vriend,

Waar is 't wonder dan
Dat twee levenslang gescheidnen
Nochtans levenslang verenen kan.
Waar is 't wonder dan?

Iedre zin is vreemd.
't Zij zo: in ons beider denken
Niets dat naar 't gedenk van de andre zweemt.
Iedre zin is vreemd.

Maar zijn vorm bekoort.
Iedre toonval vast verstaanbaar,
Iedre lijn en schakeling en woord.
Zie, zijn vorm bekoort.

Meer dan zin en geest,
Als aan de uiting voor-geboren,
Leeft in ons de Vorm, de ziele-leest,
Meer dan zin en geest.

Deze zien we aldoor,
In zich onze vreemdheid dragend,
Maar ons bindend aan zijn eigen gloor.
Deze zien we aldoor.

Vorm aan vorm verwant
Heffen zich twee vreemdling-zielen
Aan de kimmen elk van 't eigen land –
Vorm aan vorm verwant.

Noem het liefde of haat:
Siddrend groeten bij elkander,
Daar hun open oog elks vorm verstaat.
Noem het liefde of haat.

O, my dearest friend,
Clasping me whom you'd wish different,
Me who smile as over me you bend,
O my dearest friend,

Where's the wonder then
That will join two lifelong parted,
So that lifelong yet they are as one,
Where's the wonder then?

Every thought is strange.
Be it so: in either's thinking
Nothing that will fit the other's range.
Every thought is strange.

But their form will charm.
Every modulation firmly ringing,
Every line and link and very name.
See, their form will charm.

More than sense and mind,
As though born before the utterance
Lives in us that Form, that inner Kind,
More than sense and mind.

This we always see,
Bearing in itself our strangeness,
And yet joining us within its ray.
This we always see.

Form akin to form
Rise erect two stranger-souls
Each one on the borders of his home –
Form akin to form.

Call it love or hate:
Trembling they behold each other,
Since their forms in every fibre meet.
Call it love or hate.

Waar duizendvormig bladgewemel
Wiegt in een stralend blauwe hemel
Omvangt ons tent van zand en groen.
In zoete en orgelende tonen
Slingren de vogels die hier wonen
Hun liedren door 't verrukt plantsoen.

In 't eindloos spel van zang en luister
Stemt in zijn eigen schemerduister
Ons hart aldoor zijn zelfde snaar.
Vormen en volten worden dromen
En in één glimlach opgenomen
Van uw gelaat, Alzegenaar.

1–10 June 1919

Ik sloeg mijn armen uit...

Ik sloeg mijn armen uit en meende
Er u te omvangen, louter licht,
Maar eensklaps, aan mijn wangen, weende
Een droef en menslijk aangezicht.

En van verwezen lippen dropten
Mijn woorden troostend in haar haar,
Mijn polsen die van deernis klopten
Voelden haar armen mat en zwaar.

Tot liefde door haar leed bewogen
Vergat ik wens en werk en u
En vond, verdwaasd van mededogen,
Haar last niet zwaar, de weg niet ruw,

Tot aan mijn hof, tot op mijn drempel.
Daar stond ze en wenkend noodde ik: kom.
Glans laaide en 't huis straalde als een tempel
Toen ge ingingt in uw heiligdom.

17 October 1919

Where thousand-shaped the foliage trembling
Sways in a sky of radiant blue
Shades us our tent of green on sand.
The birds that in these groves are dwelling
Their sweet and warbling notes are pealing
Through the enraptured summer-land.

In endless play of song and sparkle
Our hearts within their dusky darkness
Ever attune their selfsame string.
Forms of humanity grow slumbrous
Enveloped in one smile penumbrous:
Thy countenance, all-blessing King.

I opened wide my arms…

I opened wide my arms, believing
I was embracing thee, sheer light,
When, leaning to my cheek, a grieving
And tearful human face I met.

And from my dazed lips words were dropping,
My words of comfort, in her hair,
And pulses with compassion throbbing,
I felt her arms, how limp they were.

Moved unto love by her affliction,
Forgetting wish and work and thee,
I found, bewildered with compassion,
Her burden light, not hard the way

Unto my garden, to my dwelling.
And there she stood; I beckoned: come.
Bright splendour blazed, home shone, a temple,
When thou didst to thy sanctum come.

De schone wereld

Iedre morgen na het nachtlijk slapen
Ligt mijn wereld nieuw door mij geschapen.

Iedre dag heb ik haar weggegeven,
Telkens één dag meer van 't eigen leven.

Telkens een kortstondiger bewoner
Zie ik haar belanglozer, dus schoner.

Schoonst zal ze eenmaal zijn als ik ga scheiden
En de grenslijn wegvalt van ons beiden.

28 December 1920

De liederen van Hadewych

Jaren ver, eeuwen ver,
Zit als een grote witte vogel
Die vrouw en zingt.
Al de geslachten van strijdenden, heersenden,
Vorsten, prelaten, zijn in hun graven
En niemand telt hen, –
Zij is ondoodbaar, zij doet niet anders
Dan met de hartstocht van haar begeren
En met haar maatvol bedwang
De éne bezieling, de ondeelbaar éne,
Denken in woorden.

Wie zal het schaduwloos
Licht verbeelden?
Wie 't bovenzinlijke
In zin bepeinzen?

The beautiful world

Every morning after the night's sleeping
Lies my world new-born and in my shaping.

Each day I renounce her and am giving
One day more away of my own living.

Each time a more transient in-dweller
Seeing her more selflessly – hence fairer.

Fairest will she be when farewell's started
And the border goes that keeps us parted.

Hadewych's songs

Years away, ages away,
Sits like a great white bird
That woman, and sings.
All the generations of warriors, rulers,
Princes, prelates, are in their graves,
And no one heeds them, –
She is deathless, she strives for ever
With the passion of her desiring
And with her balanced control
To voice the one inspiration, the utterly one,
Think it in words.

Who shall picture
Shadowless light?
Who shall ponder
Supersensuous in sense?

Wanhoop bevangt haar,
Maar de Wil
Tot het Onmooglijke,
Juist deze is van edele zielen de beweegkracht:
Juist deze drijft haar zodat ze overweldigend zingt.

Niemand, zo zegt ze, kan Minne genoegdoen,
Zonder de Minne is elk leven leed,
Erger dan dood is Minneloos leven.
Minne, onthef ons aan alles wat laag is,
Minne, bedwing ons tot één met uzelf.
Eén met uzelf, ach hoe woed ik verbijsterd, –
Nochtans, wat weelde zo gij me maar wenkt.
Weelde, doch wanhoop ook: bei maken zalig.
Ach, overwin mij maar, sterkste die zijt!
Als alles vergaat rijst gij, Minne, klaarder.
Woorden beseffen niet hoe ge ons omvangt.
Eindlijk toch neigt ge u en zegt: in mijn armen,
Lieve, in mijn armen voer ik u thuis.

Zij hunkert, zij haakt
Naar die Éne.
Doel, drang en zaligheid,
Minne is het woord ervoor.
De hooggeborene
Stoutmoedige Jonkvrouw
Kan niet gedogen
Dat het hoogste denken
Haar ontgaan zou.

Zij dwingt het met voeten te treden
Op haar de verslagene,
In een roes en ontruktheid
Voelt ze zich één ermee,
Gewaart hoe het ingaat, lichaam en geest, in haar,
Schouwt en beleeft zijn bewegingen.
Maar het hoofse woord:
Maat en rijm van het ridderlijk minnelied,
Het lentelijk spel van de liefde
Op veld en in bogaard

Despair overcomes her,
But the Will
To achieve the Impossible,
This is the very impulse of noble souls:
This is what drives her, till, overwhelming, she sings:

No one, she says, can serve Love enough,
Outside Love any life is grief,
Worse than death is Love-less living.
Love, uplift us from all that is low,
Love, make us yield to thee, one with thyself.
One with thyself – ah, I rave bewildered, –
And yet, what bliss, if thou beckonest me.
Bliss, but despair too: both render blessed.
Ah, do but vanquish me, strongest who art!
When all things perish, thou, Love, risest brighter.
Words cannot fathom thy mode of embrace.
Yet at last thou bend'st over me, say'st: in my arms,
Love, in my arms I will lead thee home.

She hankers, she yearns
For that One.
Goal, urge and blessedness,
Love is her word for it.
The high-born
Stout-hearted damsel
Cannot endure
That the highest thinkable
Should escape her.

She compels it to tread underfoot
Her, the defeated one.
In a storm of ecstasy
She feels herself one with it,
Undergoes its entering, body and spirit, in her,
Beholding and feeling its movements.
But the courtly word:
Rhythm and rhyme of the chivalrous love-song,
The springtime play of love
In field and orchard

Of tussen de hagen
Kadert en doorgeurt vizioen en afgrond:
Lente wordt overal wat Minne heet.
Door haar schallende strofen,
Door de wisslende regel-maat,
Door de reiende en beurtende rijmendans,
Stroomt op haar stem en haar bloedslag
De door woord noch denking benaderde
Lichaamgeworden
Minne, de god-mens.
Deze verbeelding,
De natuurlijke,
Bevat al het bovennatuurlijk onmooglijke
Zichtbaar en blijvend,
Deze is de ware verschijning van Hadewych,
De vrouw die van Minne zong.

25 January 1920

De legenden van de ene weg
25 July – 11 August 1920

Het sterrenbeeld

Het dal was donker en de weg was eng,
Hij wist dat uit de ruigten slangen loerden,
De hemel was een dunne en bleke streep.

Hij was gedaald: nu steeg hij, slank en streng,
Alsof de stenen hem naarboven voerden,
Een knods van wingerd hield zijn vaste greep.

En toen het scheen alsof op hoogste rand
Zich ogen brandend in de zijne boorden,
Hij toeslaan wilde op 't monster dat hem zocht,

Zag hij, zich neigend van de hemelwand
't Gesternte slingren, dat zijn gulden koorden,
Een labyrinth van licht, rondom hem vlocht.

Or among the brushwood
Frames and lends fragrance to vision and abyss:
Spring grows everywhere in the world of Love.
Through her ringing stanzas,
Through the variously cadenced lines,
Through the winding and meeting dance of the rhymes
Streams on her voice and her blood-beat
The One whom neither word nor thought will convey:
The embodied
Love, the god-man.
This portrayal,
The natural one,
Embraces everything supernatural and impossible
Visible and abiding,
This is the true appearance of Hadewych,
The woman who sang of Love.

The legends of the one way

The constellation

The way was narrow and the dale was dark,
He knew that in the thickets snakes were hiding,
The heavens were a thin and glimmering line.

He had gone down; he climbed now, slender, stark,
As though the boulders sped his upward striding,
His bludgeon, firmly gripped, a trunk of vine.

And when it seemed, up on the highest rim,
As though eyes burning bored into his eyes,
– He raised his weapon for the monster's charge –,

He saw, inclining towards him from the skies,
The constellation winding, and its golden cords,
A labyrinth of light, enfolded him.

Het witte zeil

De rots schoof dicht. Als een spalier vol rozen
Rezen de bergen, hoog en eindloos ver,
Het land lag in een net van zonnevonken.

Hij die uit donker kwam bleef aarzlend pozen.
Van stroom en vogels schalde 't her en der.
Geluid en licht maakten hem stil en dronken.

Hij was geworden uit het ondergrondse
Tot de bewoner van dit tuin-heelal
En wist niet hoe; noch waar zijn schred te richten.

Toen zag hij waar de stroom de horizontse
Bergen doorsneed, ankrend voor havenwal,
Een klein schip dat zijn witte zeil deed lichten.

De brug

Zij grondden in de woeste stroom hun brug.
Maar dat er vrede en sterkte in 't steen zou wonen:
'Wiens liefste 't eerst hier komt, metsel haar in!'

De zon brandde 't gebergt op flank en rug
Toen zingend kwam wie haar gemaal zou lonen
Met vooraadvolle korf en kroes van tin.

Zij hieven haar – zijn armen hingen slap –,
Zij stelden haar in 't ruim, met voordacht open,
Zij metsten, metsten en haar blik werd groot.

Zij kreet – dit was niet meer een mannegrap! –
Hij zweeg en in haar hart verging het hopen:
Zij metsten, metsten tot de pijler sloot.

The white sail

The rock swung to. An espalier of roses,
Arose the mountains, high, immensely far;
The land lay in a net of sun-sparks sunken.

He, coming from deep darkness, wavering pauses.
Ringing of rivers, bird-song everywhere,
The sound and light making him still and drunken.

From underground existence he'd arisen
To be a dweller in this garden-sphere
And knew not how, nor where to make his way.

Then where the stream cut through the far-away
Mountains, he saw along a harbour-pier
A little ship's one white sail brightly glisten.

The bridge

They braved the raging stream to found their bridge.
But so that peace and strength should fill the stone:
'Whose love shall come here first, let's brick her in!'

The sun grew burning on hillside and ridge –
Singing she came who would reward her man
With rich-stored basket and full mug of tin.

They lifted her – his arms were hanging limp –,
They placed her in the space, on purpose open,
They mortared, mortared, and aghast she gazed.

She screamed – this jest of men was growing grim! –
He stood dumb, in her heart perished the hoping:
They mortared, mortared till the pillar closed.

De vogel

In de oude boom fluisterde de Dryade.
Een vogel, blauw en goud, streek neer in 't loof:
Hij kwam door de ether, uit een ver vreemd land.

'Hij leeft door mij, ik gaf hem de genade
Dat hij nog groent. Hij kerkert me en is doof
Voor 't fluistren achter die onduldbre wand.'

De vogel zei: 'Ik kwam vandaag in 't reizen
De zon voorbij: hij zond zijn stralen uit
Van ster tot ster naar deze jeugdige aard,

En wáár hij scheen, ontloken paradijzen,
Gediert bewoog, kleur schoot in bloem en kruid:
Hij enkel wekte 't groen in dit geblaart.'

De gestorvenen

Wij voeden daaglijks met ons bloed de geesten
Van de gestorvenen, die in ons wonen:
Zij hebben aan ons doen en lijden deel.

Hun strijd is de onze en achter onze feesten
Is hun stille bestaan troosten of honen,
Hun adem klopt in 't lied uit onze keel.

Maar zij zijn blind. Wij hebben de ogen open
En 't heel heelal is in hun straal ons eigen,
Wij zien de wegen gaan van ster tot ster.

Deze zijn de onze en deze te belopen
Maakt de verrukkingen van 't droomzwaar zwijgen
Dat geesten doen, klaarder en lieflijker.

The bird

In the old tree the Dryad's whisper sighs.
A bird, blue-gold, lighted among the leaves:
It came through the ether, from a strange far land.

'It lives through me, 't was I gave it the grace
That keeps it green. It dungeons me and leaves
Unheard my whispers in this prison penned.'

And the bird said: 'This morning as I journeyed
I passed the sun, and he sent out his rays
From star to star down to this youthful earth,

And where he shone, paradise-gardens burgeoned,
The creatures moved, bright flowers and plants arose:
By him alone were these green leaves called forth.'

The departed

We daily nurture with our blood the spirits
Of the departed, who in us live on:
They share in all we do and all we bear.

Their fight is ours and deep behind our cheer
Their still existence stands – comfort or scorn.
What our voice sings, their breath in us inspirits.

But they are blind. Our eyes are open, keen,
The universe within their gaze is ours,
We see the ways that lead from star to stars.

These ways are ours, and along these our course
Renders the raptures of their dream-weighed hours
For silent spirits sweeter and more serene.

De gerichte wil

Wanneer ik stierf en zij die mij beminden
Rondom mijn baar staan en de een d'andre vraagt:
Wat hadt ge lief in hem: zijn menslijkheid,

Zijn dichterlijke gaaf, zijn trouw aan vrinden,
De zachtheid van een kracht die draagt en schraagt,
Of de onafhanklijkheid van zijn beleid, –

Dan hoop ik dat een zeggen zal: wij weten
Dat hij als mens, dichter en vriend, als kracht
En leider 't zijne deed, maar nu de spil

Van 't denken stilstaat en in zelfvergeten
Zijn mond zich sloot, zien wij zijn sterkste macht:
Een op de onsterflijkheid gerichte wil.

Rijpheid

'Eusebia, laat los!' Die kreet van Vondel
Toen hij vooraanging in het vast besluit
Voortaan alleen te leven als gewijde

En lust en leed, te lang gedragen bondel,
Afwierp, opdat zijn geest, door niets gestuit,
De klaarheid won waar hij zich heel bevrijdde,

Die kreet klinkt weer wáár eedlen, rijp en ouder,
De wereld weten, en hun liefst geloof
Vervolgen willen op gedroomde bergen.

Zij voelen vleugels wassen aan hun schouder
En zijn voor 't schreien van de harten doof
Die hun de vreugd van 't dal nog eenmaal vergen.

The directed will

When I have died and those who loved me stand
Around my bier, when maybe one will ask:
'What did you love in him: his human-kindness,

His poet's gift, his faithfulness to friends,
The gentle strength that bears and shares distress,
The vision wherewith he performed his task,' –

Then one, I hope, 'we know indeed' will answer,
'That as man, poet, friend, and as a guide,
A force, he did his part; but now that still

The wheel of thought stands and in self-surrender
His mouth has closed, we see his strongest might:
One aim, immortal Life, inspired his will.'

Maturity

'Eusebia, let go!' That cry from Vondel
As he forged onward with the firm decree
Henceforth to live alone and dedicated,

Having shed griefs' and pleasures' long-borne bundle,
So that his spirit, now entirely free,
Might win the clarity that liberated,

That cry is heard again where poets, older,
Mature, have known the world, and will pursue
Their chosen faith on visionary heights.

They feel how wings are growing from their shoulder,
Deaf to the weeping hearts that fain would sue
Them to enjoy once more the vale's delights.

Orfeus

Had Orfeus niet Eurydice gedood
Door zelf te hunkren naar haar levende ogen,
Voor eeuwig had hij haar in 't licht gevoerd.

Nu stond hij wenend waar zich de afgrond sloot
En had voorgoed zich aan zijn arm onttogen
Wie hij zo vast zich dacht aan 't hart gesnoerd.

Nu bleef zijn hunkren als een open wond
En 't lied van nederwaarts gericht verlangen
Zwaar en verzadigd, als een boom die treurt,

Terwijl die Andre opnieuw de cirkling bond
Waaruit alleen de opvaart van zijn gezangen
Haar – voor hoe kort, helaas! – had losgescheurd.

De stijgende kracht

Mijn kracht, verzameld tot een effen meer,
Zal niet de tuinen in de laagte drenken
Maar enkel de hoogstijgende fontein.

Als ik mijn ogen naar de bergen keer
Is 't of de stralen mij als sterren wenken
En ik in hen 't uitspansel nader schijn.

Maar als hun droppling sprenkelt in het dal
En iedre bloem zich opheft in de gaarde
En vogels tjilpen in 't bevocht prieel,

Dan voel ik met een hart vol hemelval
Mij kind en heer van een gelukkige aarde
En luister naar haar dank waarin ik deel.

Orpheus

If Orpheus had not killed Eurydice
By wanting for himself her living eyes,
For ever he'd have raised her to the light.

Now he stood weeping where earth closed, and she
Had for all time withdrawn from his embrace
Whom he thought clasped so firmly to his heart.

Now yearning stayed with him, an open wound,
And the laments of downward-reaching longing,
Drooping and heavy, were like trees that mourn,

Whereas that Other One was once more bound
In the orbit from which by his soaring singing
– Ah, for how short a span! – she had been torn.

Soaring strength

My strength, gathered into a level lake,
Shall not assuage the gardens in the valley
But only feed the fountain soaring high.

When with my eyes the mountain-range I seek,
The jets of water, starlike, seem to draw me,
Until in them I seem nearer the sky.

But as their droplets sprinkle down on earth
And flowers lift up their faces in the dell
And birds are twittering in the moistened bower,

Then, my heart full of what from heaven fell,
I feel both child and lord of joyous Earth
And listen to her thanks in which I share.

Eva

Toen God-zelf omging door het Paradijs
'Ik groet u dochter!' klonk zijn groet tot Eve.
Hoe anders klonk daarna het slanggeluid!

'Gij zult gelijk aan God zijn, even wijs,
En niet een kind dat voor zijn Schepper beve,
Zo ge eet van deze vrucht, uw zoete buit.'

En ze at. En Adam at. En 't vurig zwaard
Dreef beiden naar een rijk van rots en doornen:
Hem die een god scheen, en haar, nog een kind.

Dat Moeder werd, die Kaïn heeft gebaard
En Abel, tot ellende en dood geboornen.
En Gods stem klonk niet langer in de wind.

Afstand

Wie rijst ziet de aardse cirkel telkens wijder
En ruimer geördend land en zee daarin.
Hij kent zijn lieven elk op de eigen plaats.

Hij de Bevrijde wenkt hen als Bevrijder
En in hun hart ontwaakt een nieuwe zin
Voor de orde omhoog die zich omlaag weerkaats'.

Omlaag de volte, omhoog het eindloos open
Maar waarin elk die 't vindt elks ogen lokt.
En straal- en doelpunt wordt hij voor hun blik.

Dan daalt de ruimte en 't is als een ontknopen
Van strik en banden die ge rond u trokt.
En afstand wordt op 't woord: daar gij, hier ik.

Eve

When God himself would walk in Paradise
'I greet thee, daughter!' rang his hail to Eve.
How otherwise sounded the Serpent's strain!

'Thou shalt be like the Lord God, be as wise,
Not, trembling child, unto thy Maker cleave,
If of this fruit thou eatest, thy sweet gain.'

She ate. And Adam ate. The fiery sword
Drove both into a realm of rock and thorn:
Him who seemed godlike, and her, still a child.

Who grew to be a Mother and who bore
Abel and Cain, to death and sorrow born.
And God's voice rang no longer in the wild.

Distance

Who rises sees earth's circle ever wider,
More amply ordered lands' and seas' expanse.
He knows his loved ones each in his abode.

He, liberated, beckons them as Liberator,
And in their hearts there wakens a new sense
Of order, seen on high, pursued below.

Below's the throng, on high immense the space,
But whither each who finds draws each one's gaze,
An aim and focal point for every eye.

Then space descends, as though you did unlace
The knots and ties wherewith you hemmed your ways.
Distance ensues the word: there you, here I.

De Heerser

Het leven is een schone en bloedige strijd
Waar alle om de oppermacht elkaar bevechten,
Maar grootste zegen is een vast bestuur.

Ik zie de woeling die zich wild verwijdt,
Maar in een Hand die wijs en sterk zal rechten
Hangt roerloos brandend de onafwendbare Uur.

De Heerser komt: zijn Vrede is niet de dood,
Maar de ongerechtigheid van 't tweevoud leven
Verslonden in een breukloos-rein bestaan.

Hij is die de Oorsprong ons weer opensloot.
De waan van Tweeheid heeft hij uitgedreven.
De Scheppings-daad heeft hij opnieuw gedaan.

De gevangene

Gij moet niet wachten tot ik kom.
Ik ben gekerkerd en geboeid.
Maar vensters heb ik om en om
En zie hoe alles groeit en bloeit.

Ik zag uw opvlucht uit de stroom
En naar de bergen op de kim:
Uw licht lag als een sluierzoom
Op 't pad dat ik met ogen klim.

Toen rees een grote en rode maan
En bloesems blonken in haar glans.
Ik heb lang aan een raam gestaan
En warm geluk vulde mij gans.

Gij moet niet komen als ik roep:
Ik spreek soms luid voor mij alleen.

The Ruler

Life is a beautiful and blood-stained war
Where all fight others for consummate power,
But greatest blessing is a steady rule.

I see wild welter spreading wide and far,
But in a wise Hand that shall judge and rule
Hangs moveless burning the predestined Hour.

The Ruler comes: his Peace does not bring death,
But the unrighteousness of twofold life
Drowned in a mode flawlessly pure and true.

He our First Origin re-openeth.
He ousts the phantom of twin natures' strife.
Creation's act by him is done anew.

The prisoner

You must not wait until I come.
I'm fettered in an iron room.
But I have windows all around
And see how all things grow and bloom.

I saw you rise up from the stream
Towards the distant mountains' line
Your light fringed like a veiling gleam
The path that with the eyes I climb.

Then there arose a great red moon
And in its radiance blossoms showed.
I long gazed from a window then,
Warm happiness within me glowed.

You must not come when I call out:
I may speak for myself alone.

Mijn denken draagt mij als een sloep:
Gij staat aan de oever op een steen

En reikt me uw hand, maar als ik grijp
Werpt mij een plotselinge schok
Terug en in mijn handen nijp
Ik staaf of tralie van mijn hok.

Maar mijn geluk is even groot,
Het is de wereld die ik weet,
Die buiten me en die 'k in mij sloot:–
Eén wereld, – die ik de uwe heet.

Ik zeg u nu mijn diepst geheim:
Het schijnt dat ik gevangen ben,
Maar ik ben zelf 't ommuurde heim
Dat alles insluit wat ik ken.

21–22 July 1921

Roepen uit de diepte

1

Uit mijn ellende
Roep ik tot u.
Voor ik u kende
Kreet ik als nu.

Hongrende zinnen
Drinken uw dag,
Denkingen spinnen
U in hun rag.

Eén ding daarneven
Blijft mij ontzegd:
U, o mijn leven!
Dienen als knecht.

My thinking bears me like a boat:
You stand on shore upon a stone,

And stretch your hand, but as I seize
I'm thrown back with a sudden shock
Into my cell, and what I squeeze
Proves only prison-bar or lock.

But I am full of happiness:
It is the world I've always known,
Which both outside and in me lies: –
One world, – and which I call your own.

I'll say my deepest secret now:
I seem imprisoned in a room,
But I'm myself the walled-in home
Enclosing everything I know.

Calling from the depths

1

Out of my anguish
I call to you.
Ere I knew you
I cried as now.

Hungering senses
Drink in your day,
Thinking is spinning
You in its fray.

One thing beyond it is
Always denied:
Serve you, my life!, and
Stand by your side.

IJver verteert me,
Doelloze wil
Vat en doorspeert me,
Rad om zijn spil.

Zinneloos wentlen!
Wegloze reis!
Nergens een kentlen
Buiten mijn kreis!

2

O bitterheid, dat als ik sta
En met een schreeuw de stilte splijt,
Ik mij op anders niets berâ
Dan op doelloos- en ledigheid.

En dat ben ik, die levenslang
Van u mijn taak en opgaaf kreeg,
Nooit hunkerde in verlaten drang,
Nooit vruchtloos om een uitweg heeg.

En dat zijt gij, die voor elk wicht
Een weg weet waar het dartlen kan,
Door wie elk dier juist dat verricht
Waartoe het al zijn krachten spann'.

Mij laat ge als Petrus zijn die jong
Kon gaan en doen zoals hij wou,
Maar die men oudgeworden dwong
Te doen wat hij niet wou, maar zou.

Mij erger; want uw dwang op mij
Is dat ik zit en niets moet doen,
Terwijl ik wenste, één amerij,
De riem te ontknopen van uw schoen.

Ardour devours me,
Aimless will
Seizes and spears me,
Shaft through my wheel.

Senseless my turning!
Nowhere bound!
Never a swerving
Out of my round!

2

O bitterness, that as I stand
And as my cry then cleaves the peace,
I ponder not a single trend
But aimlessness and idleness.

And such am I, who from life's morn
Received from you my call and task,
Who never yearned and starved forlorn,
Nor vainly for your help would ask.

And such are you, who for each child
Can find a place of joy and light,
Through whom each creature of the wild
Can work its will with all its might.

My lot's like Peter's, who when young
Could go and do just as he would,
But old and having served so long
Must do not what he would, but should.

My lot is worse; for you command
Me to sit still and nothing do,
Whereas I long just once to bend
Before you and unloose your shoe.

3

En nu, juist nu, heb ik mijn kracht
Gespannen tot de laatste dracht,
Opdat ik de allerzwaarste vracht
Mocht dragen.

Mijn lege handen hef ik hoog,
O of ge u uit uw toren boog,
Tot ik door bidden u bewoog
En klagen!

Maar gij blijft stil en toont u niet,
Al weet ik dat uw oog mij ziet,
Al galmt mijn hart, dat gij gebiedt,
Uw slagen....

Gij zijt in mij: ik sloot u in!
Gij waart in mij, van aanbegin!
Tot eeuwigheid maakte uw gewin
Mijn dagen!

27–29 May 1922

Het ontwaken

Dat ik u liefhad hebt ge altijd geweten,
Maar nu de schaduw van de berg zich lengt,
Vergun me een vraag. Toen onze reis begon
Was ik bij 't opgaan van de zon
Aan 't zeestrand op het vlakke zand gezeten.
Daar zag ik u, het been door schuim besprengd,
D sterke heupen, de opgebogen borsten,
De haren die maar net niet vallen dorsten:
Hun blonde wrong hing in uw hals. Ik heb vergeten
Hoe toen uw naam was, maar het was een blijde.
Nu heet ge Leed. Hoe kan dat? En zij zeide
Eerst niets; doch toen: Tevoren heette ik Vreugde,
Nu Leed: maar eer we aan 't eind van gindse heide
De Nacht gestrekt zien in 't woestijnzand, noemen
Uw lippen de andre naam, die u niet heugde.

3

And now, just now, I have at length
Strained utterly my utmost strength,
To lift the greatest heaviest weight
And bear it.

High have I raised my empty hands;
O would that from your tower you bent
Until my prayer made you relent
And hear it!

But you stay still, and never show,
Although your eye sees *me*, I know,
And my heart throbs, obeying you,
Your beats....

You are in *me*, enclosed within!
You were in me, since I began!
Eternity you gave me in
My days!

The awakening

That I have loved you, you have always known,
But as the shadow of the mountain lengthens,
I'd wish to ask you.... When our course began
– It was the rising of the sun –
By the sea-shore on flat sand I was sitting.
And there I saw you, legs all splashed with foam,
Your strong hips, upward curving breasts,
Your hair that only just fell short of tumbling,
Its golden coil hung in your neck. – I have forgotten
What name was yours then, but it was a blithe one.
Now it is Grief. How can that be? And she
At first said nothing; then: I once was Joy,
Now Grief; but ere, where yonder moorlands end,
We see the night outstretched on desert sand,
Your lips will form the name you can't remember.

En in haar woorden klonk een donker roemen.
Wij gingen voort. Toen heb ik 't hoofd geheven.
Ik zag haar nauw. Ik zei: Gij zijt het Leven.

Gij zijt het Leven, zei ik. En zij lachte
Bevrijdend. Weet ge 't weer? Al mijn gedachte
Was altoos u die naam te doen onthouden.
Gij moogt me als Vreugd liefhebben of als Leed, –
Ik ben die, – maar ten laatste weten mijn Vertrouwden
Hoe ik waarlijk heet.
In de ene en de andere gedaante dragen
Mijn leden de éne godlijkheid.
Al naar ik u door licht of schaduw leid
Verschaf ik u verrukkingen of plagen.
Ik moet u altijd vragen
In mijn gelaat te zien en daar te lezen.
Bedroefd of blij bewaar ik 't zelfde wezen.
Of langs ze een glimlach of een schreien glijdt,
Het blijven de eigen ondoorgrondelijke trekken
Waarin ge 't woordloos luistren zult ontdekken
Dat alle weten begeleidt.
Zie mij nu aan! – En in die schemer groeiden
Haar voorhoofd en haar ogen en haar leden.
Zij was geen vrouw meer, maar een sterrennacht, gegleden
Over een sluimrende aarde. Ik lag beneden
Haar blikken. Geen gedachten moeiden
Zich in mij; maar ik wist dat de gewaden
Waardoor zij Leed of Vreugd was, niet meer golden;
En dat nochtans, zo wijd er zonnen rolden
Door het verrukkelijk heelal, geen daden
Bestaan dan hare. Ik hield mijn ogen dicht
En dacht te sterven. Maar een zacht gestreel
– Het duingras? – deed me ontwaken.
Een vogel klapwiekte uit het naast struweel.
Boven me 't blauw, rondom me 't middaglicht
Op struik en helm, lager het felle blaken
Van zon op zand. De zee lag in zijn perk
Te deinen, en mij lokte in 't hart het Werk.

17 September 1922

And as she spoke her voice was dusky glory.
We wandered onward. Then I raised my head
And said – I barely saw her –, You are Life.

You're Life, I said again. Her laughter
Gave freedom. Do you *know* again? My striving
Was always that you should recall that name.
You may love me as either Joy or Grief, –
I am those, – but at last my trusted friends
Know my true name.
In one form and the other do my limbs
Embody one divinity.
As I lead you through light or through the shadows
I shall enrapture you or plague you.
I always have to make you
Gaze in my eyes, that you may read what's there.
For, sad or glad, I stay the self-same being.
Whether a smile glide o'er them or a tear,
Mine will remain the same unfathomed traits
In which you'll always find the wordless listening
That with all knowledge goes.
Look in my eyes! – And in the gloaming rose
Her forehead and her eyes, her very limbs.
She was no longer woman – starry night
Gliding above a slumbering earth. I lay
Beneath her gaze. No thoughts were moving
Within me; but I knew now that the garments
That made her Grief or Joy, no more obtained;
And that beyond, as wide as suns revolve
Through the resplendent universe, nothing is,
But is through her. I lay there, still, eyes closed,
Seemingly dying. But a soft caress –
The dune-grass? – made me waken.
A bird flap-winged its way from a near bush.
Over me blue, around me mid-day light
On shrubs and marram, lower the dazzling blaze
Of sun on sand. The sea before me surged
Immensely, and an impulse stirred my heart: the Work.

De bedelaar

Wij zijn tot de eigen stilte
Teruggekeerd
Waarin wij eens ons wonen in dit land begonnen.
Toen was mijn nood het leven dat ik liet:
De vrees dat het met onvoorzien gevolg,
Of als erinring, of als ingeschapen
Ritmische kreisloop en noodlottige
Herhaling van zichzelf, mijn nieuw bestaan
En werk zou storen.
Nu is mijn nood een andre: ik heb gedaan
Wat ik toen droomde:
Mijn leven heb ik als een stad gebouwd
Met toegangen en poorten; brede straten
Monden in pleinen; parken overhuiven
De eeuwige stroom; mijn berg rijst hoog en steil
En van zijn hellingen zie ik de wereld,
De grenzenloze, en een gezegend volk
Bewoont de huizen en beweegt en werkt.
Maar op de berg bouwde ik mijn hoogste huis,
Mijn kathedraal, het standbeeld van mijn Heer.
Hoe zal ik gaan, nu ik tot daartoe klom,
En knielde,
Hoe zal ik gaan tot wie ik ginds bemin,
Al de gedachten van mijn jongre tijd?

Of moeten gij en ik, alleen, naar de andre zijde
De hellingen begaan,
En weten dat ook daar een wereld wacht?
Het is het land van de ondergaande zon
Dat nu zich uitstrekt, onbebouwd en breed.
Kom mee, nog altijd draag ik in mijn hand
Het speeltuig dat de stenen schikt.
In de uwe draagt ge
De lamp van 't brandend hart.
Ook als de nacht valt kan het, om ons beiden heen,
Niet donker zijn.
Wij zullen enkel, van omlaag gezien,
Een geheimzinniger paar, in schemerkloven,

The beggar

Into that very stillness
We have returned
In which long since our dwelling in this land began.
Then my anxiety was the life I'd left:
The fear that, with an unforeseen result,
Whether remembered, or through an inborn
Rhythmical cycle and a fatal
Comeback to itself, it would disturb
My new life and my work.
Now my anxiety is different: I have done
What then I dreamed:
My life now is a city I have built
With entrances and gateways; the broad streets
Lead into squares; parks overshadow
The eternal stream; my mountain rises high and steep
And from its sloping sides I see the world,
The boundless one, in which a blessèd people
Dwell in the houses, move around and work.
But on the mountain stands my highest house,
My great cathedral, statue of my Lord.
How shall I go, now I have climbed to there,
And knelt,
How shall I go towards my loved ones yonder,
To all the thoughts I had in younger days?

Or must we, you and I, alone, on yonder side
Tread downward slopes,
Knowing that also there a world awaits us?
It is the country of the setting sun
That now is stretching, buildingless and broad.
Come with me, for I still bear in my hand
The lyre that builds and orders stones.
In yours you bear the
Lamp of the burning heart.
Even when night falls, we two cannot be
In utter darkness.
Only, as seen from down below
We'll be a more mysterious pair, in twilight chasms,

De toovnaars van de neergang, wondren werken
Op alle paden.
De stroom breekt onder ons zijn diepre bed,
Zijn net van sterren spant de hemel uit
En de uit de grond gezongen bouw strekt neer
Langs onverbiddelijker lijnen
Van wet die wij beluistren.
Ik geloof
Dat nooit nog in 't heelal zo zeekre gevels
Verrezen, nooit zich spanningen
Van koepels zo geweldig wijdden
Als waar de Nacht nabij was.
Ik weet:
Sterkste van architecten is de Stilte.

'Gij zult veel eerder, blijvende op uw berg,
Gelijk Elia door een vuurge wagen
Worden gehaald.
Nochtans, mijn Vriend, ik die u begeleidde
Tot hier, weet beter waar uw hart naar dringt.
Gij hoort tot hen die in de hemel zelfs
Niet altijd willen wonen, maar verkiest
De troeble wereld, de vernedering,
Het afstand doen van roem die ge verkreegt,
't Veelvoudig huwlijk, en de menslijkheid.
Zie naar uw volk: het heeft maar één geloof:
Dat niemand voor zichzelf is, en hun koning
Met allen samen, en meteen hun slaaf,
En ieder slaaf en koning.
Zodra ge u losmaakt uit hun ring, ontstijgt
In stralen of u katakomben bouwt
Naar een verborgen einder,
Schokt hun gemeenschap, wordt hun heel bestaan
Onwezenlijk.
Er is geen weg dan tussen hen en u.'
Ik haalde dieper adem toen zij zweeg
En wendde me om.
Ik zal omlaag gaan, zei ik, maar niet reizend
Als wie zijn stad verlaat.

Magicians of descent who're working wonders
On all the paths.
The stream beneath us breaks its deeper bed,
A net of stars is spread over the heavens
And downwards stretch the song-created buildings
Along still sterner lines
Of law which we obey.
I believe
That never anywhere such firmly founded gables
Have risen, never such tense structures
Of domes expanded so tremendous
As where the Night was near.
I know:
Strongest of architects is Stillness.

'Far sooner will you stay upon your mountain
And, like Elijah, on a fiery chariot
Be taken hence.
And yet, my Friend, as your companion
Thus far, I know much better what your heart desires.
You're one of those who even in Heaven
Would not for ever dwell, but you prefer
The turbid world, humiliation,
Renunciation of the glory you have won,
The marriage with all life; humanity.
Look at your people: theirs is but one faith:
That no-one is his own, and that their king
Shares with them all, and also is their slave,
And each both slave and king.
Once you detach yourself, rise from their midst
In rays of light, or build your catacombs
Towards an end yet hidden,
Their fellowship is shattered, their existence grows
Phantasmal.
There is no way but between them and you.'
I breathed more deeply as she ceased
And turned about.
I will go downwards, said I, but not going
Like one who leaves his town.

Ik zal nog eenmaal onder al de mijnen
De minste zijn.
Uw woorden hebben mij opnieuw geboren.

De klokken luidden toen ik onbemerkt
Trad in de volte. Ik droeg een beedlaarspij
En hief mijn hand waarin elk zonder zien –
Want elk schreed snel en zocht zijn werk – de gift
Liet vallen die ik eertijds schonk.
Ik werd al sterker, ziend elks blij gelaat
En dat mij geen herkende. Ik zette op 't marktplein
Mij aan de bron en dacht: Leef voort, mijn volk;
Ik ben de onzichtbre band waardoor gij zijt,
Van uw gebouwen 't schijnloze cement,
De toon die uit uw klokken klinkt –
Ik ben de ontvangende van uw weldadigheid:
Geef, geef!
En als de dropplen die uit hun fontein
Stegen en stortten, zó was over mij
Van dag tot dag, hun geven.
Mij, hun beedlaar,
Gaf elk, en geen kende voortaan zijn stad
Zonder haar beedlaar.
En niemand wist dat hij de koning was.

29 – 30 March 1924

Een dag in April

Onder een grijze hemel
Waarin het licht, gelijk een ademhalen,
Nu mindert en dan zwelt,
En als het door wil breken
Weer langzaam mindert,
Ligt de nog naakte polder, met zijn weiden
En tuinen, in dit vroeg begin
Van 't voorjaar.

Once more I will be among all my own
The very least.
Your words have caused me to be born again.

The bells were ringing as I, unobserved,
Mixed with the throng. I wore a beggar's cape,
Held out my hand and, without looking at me –
For everyone strode swiftly to his work – each gave
The gift I'd once conferred on him.
I all along grew stronger, seeing each glad face,
And recognised by no one. In the market-place
I sat down by the spring and thought: Live on, my people,
I am the unseen bond through which you are,
And in your buildings I'm the humble mortar,
The tone that rings from all your bells –
I'm the receiver of your charity:
Give! give!
And like the drops which always from their fountain
Rose and fell, just so was over me
From day to day, their giving.
To me, their beggar,
Everyone gave; henceforth none knew his town
Without its beggar.
And no one realised he was the king.

A day in April

Under a grey sky
In which the light, like quiet breathing,
Now wanes and then will swell
And as it's almost shining
Falls to slow waning,
Lies the still naked polder, with its meadows
And gardens, in this spare beginning
Of spring.

Een zilverige wereld die nog wacht
Dat zij een gouden wordt.
Zó is in mij een zilveren verwachting
Geweven, en na ieder stralenjaar
Hoop ik weer als een kind.
Ik ben geboren, een onsterflijk zaad
Van hoopvolle seizoenen. Het geloof
Dat mensen, gelijk bloemen,
Na een éénmalig bloeien welken
Werd mij geleerd;
Maar mijn ervaring leert dat in me 't leven
Telkens weer bloeit, en niet dan schijnbaar welkt.
Het wacht aldoor een nieuwe zomer.
Zijn aard is toekomst, ónverganklijkheid.
Mijn oudste vriend stierf met een hart en hoofd
Vol dromen en gedachten.
Van 't welken van zijn lichaam wist hij niets.
Niet anders dan mijn jongste, die de pen
Een oogwenk neerlei, peinzende op 't vervolg,
En niet ontwaakte.
Dit is geen loochning van het lichaam, dat zijn duur
Als andre schepslen heeft,
Maar een erkenning van het Wonder.
Wij die het sterven weten, kennen 't niet.
Wij leven in het leven, en verstaan
Zijn stem alleen, die als een eindeloze
Belofte ons naar de lippen welt.
Er was een jongling
Die met zijn laatste kracht mij zijn verrukking uitte
Dat hem een hemel wachtte
Van onuitspreekbre zaligheid, door leed
Noch zorg gestoord.
Lach niet, zei hij, want dit is geen verbeelding,
Maar werklijkheid.
Het was de stem van 't leven, dat in hem
Bij 't naadren van zijn grootste lichaamsnood,
In vormen die die jongling best verstond,
Zijn laatste waarheid zei: niet slechts Ik ben,
Maar Ik zal zijn en Ik zal reiner zijn
En heerlijker dan ooit.

A silvery world that's waiting still to grow
Into a golden one.
Só there's in me a silver expectation
Arisen: after every radiant year
I hope again like a child.
I have been born as an immortal seed
Of hopeful seasons. The belief
That human beings, like flowers,
After one season's blooming wither
Was taught me once;
But my experience shows that life within me
Will often bloom, and merely seems to wilt.
It evermore awaits another summer.
By nature it's 'to come', it cannot end.
My eldest friend died with a heart and head
Full of ideas and dreams,
Quite unaware of his own body's wilting.
And no more was my youngest, who laid down
His pen a while, thinking of what came next,
And did not waken.
This denies not our body, which has its span
As that of other creatures,
But it acknowledges a Wonder.
We who do know of dying, know it not.
We live in life, and only understand
Life's voice, as, like a never-ending
Promise it wells up towards our lips.
There was a youth
Who with his ultimate strength expressed to me his rapture
On what was coming to him: a heaven
Of bliss unspeakable, and marred
By neither grief nor care.
No, do not smile, he said, because this is not fancy,
But real truth.
It was the voice of life, which then in him
On the approaching of his body's greatest stress
Spoke to that youth in forms he understood
Its ultimate truth: not just 'I am',
But 'I shall be and I shall be more pure
And glorious than ever.'

Van dat ik jong was zingt het zó in mij
En wil niet einden.
Een oud man! zeggen er, en schoon mijn haren
Maar weinig grijzen, weet ik nu toch wel
Dat de lichamelijke winter komt.
Maar in mijn hart is lente. Ik wacht alweer
De sterrelende bloesem op mijn boom,
Het brokklen van mijn grond om 't zwellend zaad.
Volheid van leven, onweerhoudbre groei
Doordringt me en als een god van zon en dauw,
Door een prieel omloverd,
Verberg ik mij.
Is dit dan dood, dat in zijn eindlijk uur
De god in ons, onvindbaar voor onszelf,
Schuilt in zijn woud, een wereld, en de paden
Van aard naar hemel wentlen om zijn hart?

6 April 1924

De Ene

E chi mi vede, e non se n'innamora,
D'amor non averà mai intelletto.
DANTE

Ik heb u altijd met mijn lijf
Beschut, en wie mij zien gebaren
Weten niet hoe ik ben voor u.
Zo rijzen stug en wreed de vestingmuren
Waarbinnen zich 't Alhambra bergt:
Fontein en hoven en de koele zaal.

Ik heb mijn kracht verteerd in die bescherming,
Ik heb de haat van allen getrotseerd,
Ik heb mijn geest geslepen tot het web
Van stratagemen dat niet mij
Maar u onwondbaar maakt.

From youth it has been singing so in me,
· And knows no ending.
'An old man' – people say, and though my hair
Greys only slightly, yet I know full well
That for my body winter's coming now.
But in my heart is spring. I await again
The starry trembling blossom on my tree,
The crumbling of my soil round swelling seed.
Fulness of life, unwithholdable growth
Pervades me, and like a god of sun and dew,
Amid a bower of foliage,
I dwell unseen.
Is this then death: that in his final hour
The god within us, hidden from ourselves,
Withdraws into his wood, a world, and that the paths
From earth towards heaven revolve around his heart?

The One

I always with my very body
Have shielded you, and those who see my bearing
Know not what I am like for you.
So harsh and cruel do the rampart walls
Rise up enclosing the secure Alhambra:
Fountain and gardens and the cooler hall.

I have worn out my strength through that protection,
I have defied the hatred of all men,
I have refined my mind into the web
Of stratagems that make not me
But you unwoundable.

Gij zijt de schoonste en waarste en liefste.
Mijn deugd is enkel dat ik u bemin.
Wie u niet kennen, honen mij en vragen:
"Zijt ge ook zo'n ridder van La Mancha?" – Waarlijk,
Ik antwoord niet: "En Dulcinea is toch de schoonste".
Geen meisje van Tolosa werd me een waan.

Er is geen werklijkheid aan u gelijk,
Springbron van leven! Wie mijn onrust kent
Moet weten dat zij enkel dán bestaat
Als ik niet in uw oog zie. Maar uw ogen,
Mijn tovenaarster, waar zie ik die niet?
Zij lachen uit de hemel, zijn op aarde
In schepsels en verschijnsels, en als 't donkert
Flonkeren ze in mijn slaap.

Er is niets dat mij baat dan uw nabijheid.
Maar meest uw spreken. Want ik vraag me vaak,
Als ik mezelf hoor fluistren, of niet gij het
Zijt die daar spreekt.
Dit is het zoetst verkeer, als ik niet weet
Of gij en ik twee zijn of een. Ik luister
En in het luistren huwt zich ziel aan ziel.

Hoe rijk zijn uw gedachten! Al mijn jaren
Hoorde ik er andere en die toch zo klaarlijk
Kwamen van u. Nog blijft dit diep geheim
Dat ge uw gedachten, sinds de tijd begon,
Geuit hebt door velen. Als gij in mij zwijgt
Lees ik de door uw volk geschrevene.

Hij had gelijk die meende: Wie u ziet
En niet bemint, heeft geen begrip van liefde.
En: haar bekoringen zijn nieuw voor de aarde
Omdat zij haar van elders zijn gekomen.
Van elders. Neen, ik zoek u niet hierboven.
Ook hemelen zijn oud. Maar wel in 't eeuwige
Elders dat pool en oorsprong is van Hier.
Gij zijt de Nieuwheid zelf, ons ingeboren.
Gij zijt de Vreugde in 't hart van 't aarde-leed.

You are the fairest, truest, dearest one.
My virtue merely lies in that I love you.
All those who know you not, will taunt me, asking:
"Art such another knight from that La Mancha?" – Truly,
I answer not: "And yet Dulcinea is the fairest."
No maiden from Tolosa is my idol-dream.

There's no reality to equal you,
Fountain of life! Who knows my restlessness
Must know that only then does it exist
When my eye meets not yours. And yet – your eyes,
My sorceress, where do I see them not?
They smile from heaven and they are on earth
In living beings, happenings, and at night
They sparkle in my sleep.

There's nothing that avails me but your nearness.
But most your speaking. For I often wonder
As I hear myself whisper, if it is not you
Who whisper then.
This is the sweetest converse, when I know not
If you and I are two or one. I listen,
And as I listen soul weds unto soul.

How rich your thoughts are! During all my years
Would I hear other ones, which yet were clearly
Coming from you. Still there's this mystery
That you have voiced your thoughts, since time began,
Through many men. When in myself you're silent,
I read those once recorded by your own.

How right was he who spoke: 'Whoever sees you
And loves you not, has no idea of love.'
Also: 'her loveliness is new to earth
Because it was from elsewhere she received it.'
From elsewhere. No, I seek you not on high.
Heavens too are old. But you *are* in the eternal
Elsewhere that is the pole and origin of Here.
You are Newness itself, that's born within us.
You are the Joy at heart of all earth's pain.

Lang niet onwillig hoorde ik naar die felle
Verdoemer, de charontische
Vijand van alle schoon-zien:
'De aarde is een hel.'
'Met in die hel een hemel' fluisterde ik, en weerde
Zijn aanklacht af? Neen, ik begrondde haar.
Temidden van de hel, de waan, de wereld,
En grond van haar noodzaaklijkheid, zijt gij!
Heil wie u weten, enig goede en ware en schone,
En werklijke.
Zij hebben in de hel hun vaste plaats
Van zaalge rust.
En Noach's duif die met de olijftak zweefde
Over de zondvloed en naar de ark
Was niet zo veilig,
Als zij, rustende in de afgrond. Zo ik ooit,
In deze chaos van mijn tijd, de moed
Liet zinken, zo ik ooit, één ogenblik,
Geloofde dat de list, de kwade trouw,
De hebzucht en de heerszucht van een bent,
U zouden overmogen, straf mij dan,
Onttrek me uw aanzijn, en stort mijzelf uit
Mijn middelpunt van vrede. Maar ik weet –

Ik weet nóg een verborgenheid.
O mijn ontzachbre vogel,
Het is uw stormvlucht die de lagen van het zwerk
Verschoof en overal de uitmiddelpuntige
Verwarring bracht vóór ge weer neerstreekt.
Ik weet uw nestlen op de golf, ik weet
In ú het onverstoorbare evenwicht.
Vergeef wat ik zo aanstonds zei.
Ik u beschermen?
Gij breidt uw vleugels over me uit: ik schuil,
Ik ben een nestjong in uw warme dons.

23 April 1924

By no means disagreeing did I hear that fierce
Condemner, the charontian
Foe of all rosy viewing:
'Earth is a hell.'
'Within that hell's a heaven,' was my whisper – warding off
His fell indictment? No, I established it.
Amid this hell, delusion, this our world,
And ground of its necessity, there is You!
Hail to all those who know you, only good and true and fair
And real one.
They have within the hell their stronghold firm
Of blessed peace.
And Noah's dove that with the olive branch
Did skim the Flood and reached the Ark
Was not as scatheless
As they are, resting in the abyss. If ever
In the mad chaos of this age, my courage
Once faltered, if I ever, for one moment,
Believed that all the cunning, the bad faith,
The greed and power-lust of a ruthless gang
Could ever overwhelm you, strike me then,
Deprive me of your presence, hurl me down
Out of my core of peace. But I do know –

I know another mystery.
O my tremendous winged one,
It is your storm-flight that once caused the welkin's layers
To shift, and everywhere brought down
Bewildering confusion, ere you lighted.
I know your nestling on the wave, I know
In *you* the stirless balance of tranquillity.
Forgive me what just now I said.
Could *I* protect you?
You spread your wings all over me: I shelter,
I am a nestling in your warming down.

Ik heb u lief

Ik wachtte u iedere avond
En telkens kwaamt ge, een nieuwe gast.
De bloemen die in de tuinen bloeiden
Zijn alle geplukt.

Nu zit ik opnieuw in de schemer
En denk: dit is de laatste maal.
Nu zal zij komen en ik niet vragen
Wie na haar komt.

Ik heb van al mijn woorden
Het eindlijk woord voor nu bewaard.
Want wat zal ik zeggen na dit éne:
Ik heb u lief.

Ik zei het vroeg in de morgen
In de tijd toen enkel morgen bestond,
Ik zei het in mijn middagjaren,
Ik zeg het nu.

Door de dag van mijn hele leven
Is dit éne woord als een zang gegaan.
Nu is het avond: alleen gelaten
Zing ik het nog.

Dat ge mij dit liet spreken:
Ik heb u lief, ik heb u lief,
Is beter dan al de grote gaven
Die ge me schonkt.

Tot al uw duizend gedaanten
Heb ik het argeloos gezegd.
Nu zeg ik het wetend tot uw laatste,
Kort vóór de nacht.

I hold you dear

I awaited you every evening,
And then you'd come, a novel guest.
The flowers that blossomed in the gardens
Have all been picked.

Now, once again in the twilight,
I think: this is the final time.
Now she'll be coming, and I won't ask her
Who'll follow her.

Of all the words I treasure
I have saved the final word for now.
For what shall I say beyond the one:
I hold you dear.

I said it in the early morning
In the time when only morning was born,
I said it in my mid-day years,
I say it now.

Throughout the day of my lifetime
This *one* word has run like a song.
Now it is evening: alone in the gloaming
I sing it still.

That you have stirred me to speaking:
I hold you dear, I hold you dear,
Is better than all the gifts, the blessings
You've granted me.

To all your forms I've encountered
I have naïvely spoken it.
Now, knowing, I say it to your last one
Towards fall of night.

Als ik uw naam mocht noemen,
Dan wist ge waarom ik nu weet.
Ge weet het en ik hoef niet spreken:
'Ik heb u lief'.

12 May 1924

De laatste psalm

Als mij de dromen begeven
En de nacht rept
Over mijn leven,
Als dan een torenklok klept
Uit de verte, zal ik zijn galm
Vertalen in een laatste psalm.
Die zal de heerlijkheid zingen
En het scheiden, –
Het geluk van de aarde, de mens en alle dingen,
De dank en het heengaan zonder benijden,
Als van een wereld die schoonst is in haar afscheidslicht.
Of dan mijn lichaam verlaten ligt
Op het kleine kerkhof onder een steen
Of, verbrand, als as en rook
Op de winden verdween,
Dan ook,
– Ik weet het – word ik niet vergeten.
Niet omdat tekens blijven of erinring duurt,
Maar omdat deze en die
Zal eten
Van de adem van mijn poëzie,
Mijn bloed en vlees, tot droom verpuurd.
Want wat is 't leven?
Een droom, op adem van gezang
Bewaard, voor kort of lang,
En uit liefde gegeven.

3 September 1926

If I were free to name you,
You would have known why now I know.
You know, and I may leave unspoken:
'I hold you dear.'*

*The poet is speaking to Love, and is at the same time speaking to the woman he is awaiting, Love's last embodiment for him. The two beings addressed are inextricably one, for the loved one, again and again throughout his life, is the very incarnation of Love, whom he can only know in and through her.

The closing psalm

When my dreams will leave me
And the night speeds
Over my being,
Then, as a tower-bell tolls
From afar, I will transform
Its ring into a closing psalm.
Therein glory will sing
And parting, –
The joy of the earth, of man, of every thing,
The thanksgiving, the going without repining,
As from a world most lovely in her parting light.
Although my body will then lie desolate
In the little churchyard under a stone,
Or, burnt to ash and smoke
On the winds will have flown,
Even then,
– I know – I shall not be forgotten.
Not because script's enduring or remembrance lasts,
But because here and there
Someone will
Eat of the breath of my song,
My blood and flesh, in dream fulfilled.
For what is 'living'?
Dream, on the breath of song
Preserved, for a while or long,
And of Love's giving.

De belofte

1

Gij heft me en zegt: 'Nu glimlach *ik*,
Nu gij uw lied gezongen hebt,
Want meer dan 't bloed dat vloedt en ebt
In u, onttoog ik aan uw blik.

Ik ben niet enkel die gij schiept
En in een eindlijke uur verlaat,
Ik ben die was en nooit vergaat
En die ge vaak in dromen riept,

Een heerser in een ander rijk
Dan dat geslacht en tijdsduur kent
Of weet van wording, bloei en end.
Leven en dood zijn daar gelijk.

Alles is leven. En ik draag
U uit de wereld van uw oog
Naar een onzichtbre, die haar boog
Niet spant naar wet van hoog en laag.'

2

Wat is dit anders dan 't geloof
Dat het bij u goed wonen blijft?
Ik ben, belijfd of onbelijfd,
Bij u, en blijf voor 't andre doof.

Gij hebt me door zo meenge droom
Uw goed- en schoonheid ingeprent,
Dat ik van deze ook mij niet wend
Hoewel ik voor zijn vreemdheid schroom.

Ik ben een mens. Ik heb alleen
Deze ogen en dit denkend brein,
Dit hele lichaam en de lijn
Van aarde en hemel om mij heen.

The promise

I

You raise me, saying: 'Now *I* smile
Now that you have sung your song;
More than the blood which flows and ebbs
In you, I've hidden from your eye.

'I am not merely one you made
And in an ultimate hour must leave,
I'm He who was and never dies,
To whom in dreams you've often called,

'A ruler in a different land
From this which knows of kin and time,
Or knows of growth, of bloom and end.
There life and death are one, the same.

'There all is life. And I will bear
You from the world your eye can see
Towards an unseen one, whose sphere
Moves not by law of high and low.'

2

What else is this if not the faith
That with you I may safely dwell?
I am, alive or outside life
With you, and to all else stay deaf.

So many dreams you've sent me, blessed
Me with your goodness, loveliness,
That from *this* dream I will not turn,
Although its strangeness makes me fear.

I am a man; I only have
These human eyes, this thinking brain,
This living body; – I feel the line
Of earth and sky enclosing me.

Ik hoor. En nu wilt gij me doof.
En spreekt mij toch in mensetaal
Van 't zinnenloze land. Ik daal
Diep in mijzelf. Dit is geloof.

3

'Dit is geloof! Omdat ge mij
– Ik u! – het heengaan niet vergunt,
Omdat ge nooit verlaten kunt
Uzelf, – ondanks het wisslend tij

'Van dood en leven, – moet ge wel
Geloven dat een leven is,
Ontdaan van dood en duisternis,
Ontheven aan de zinnen-cel,

'Geloven dat een eeuwigheid
Zich buiten tijd en ruimte welft,
En dat geen leven graven delft
Voor zich en elk die het belijdt.

'Uit dit geloof stroomde u het licht
Waardoor uw zang gelukkig maakt.
Mijn kind, uit de éne droom ontwaakt
Ziet ge mijn andere aangezicht.'

Wederzien

Het was een helder ogenblik
Zoals eens Saulus overscheen
En zoals hij toen stond, stond ik.

Gij hadt gezegd: nu ga ik heen.
De Dood zei: en zij gaat met mij.
En gij: nu laat ik u alleen.

I hear. And now you wish me deaf,
And yet tell me in human speech
Of the non-sensuous land. I reach
Deep in my being. This is faith.

3

'Yea, this is faith! Since you divide
Not from me – nor will I from you! –
Since you can never go beyond
Yourself, – despite the shifting tide

'Of death and life, – you surely must
Believe that there exists a life
That's freed from darkness and from death,
Freed from the enclosing senses' crust,

'Believe that an eternity
Arches its dome past time and space,
And that Life will not delve a grave
For Me and all who worship Me.

'This faith gave you the shining grace
By which your gladdening song will stream;
My child, awakening from life's dream
You'll see my other, greater face.'

Ultimate meeting

It was a moment's clarity
Such as once on scribe Saul had shone,
And as he stood then, so stood I.

You said to me: now I must go.
And Death said: she will go with me.
And you: I'm leaving you alone.

Maar ik, in 't licht, stond klaar en vrij
En zei: wij zien elkander weer.
De Dood heeft macht noch heerschappij.

De Dood mag doen naar zijn begeer,
Hij staat in 't teken van de tijd,
Hij weet van keer noch wederkeer.

Maar ik – dit is mijn zekerheid –
Ik leef, en weet van toen noch nu.
Ik ben een zoon van de eeuwigheid

En waar ik kom, daar vind ik u.

16 January 1931

Liederen van laatste verstaan

1   Zeegezang

Uw zacht gezang – het kwam zo vaak
Nadat uw storm zich had gelegd.
Wat ik als doelloos schomlen laak
Was uw geluk – en mij ontzegd?

Of was er ebbe en zwakheid in
En uw geluid de weergalm maar
Van wat ge in 't juichende begin
Hebt uitgeroepen vast en klaar?

Dat nog ik in die tweestrijd hang
En met een schelp mijn oor bevreê
Bewijst wel dat ik uw gezang
Grondloos beminnen moet, mijn zee.

But I, in light, stood clear and free,
Saying: and we shall meet once more.
For Death has neither power nor sway.

Death may indeed work his desire,
He is within the realm of time,
He cannot turn, return, restore.

But I – this certainty is mine –
I live, with then nor now in mind.
Son of eternity I am,

And where I go, it's you I'll find.

Songs of ultimate understanding*

1   Sea song

Your gentle song – how oft it came
Whene'er your thunder would subside.
What I as aimless surging blame,
Was it your joy – to me denied?

Or did an ebbing weakening
Reverberation reach my ear
Of what in your exultant spring
You claimed in measures firm and clear?

That I've been torn by doubt so long
And that a shell can sing me free
Betokens I must give your song
Love that is fathomless, my sea.

* Addressed to the memory of Stefan George.

2   De stem

Vergeving, o vergeving! krijt
De stem die niets meer is als stem.
Ik zoek u, ik ontbeer u zo
En de echo enkel antwoordt mij.

Wat is er tussen mij en u
Dan wat gij zwijgt en wat ik roep:
De schuld van 't nooit genoeg verstaan,
Die klaagt en zwijgt, die zwijgt en klaagt,

In 't holle graf, door 't hol gewelf
Van lege heemlen zonder hoop.
En dan een beving door 't heelal
Alsof ge nochtans hadt gehoord.

3   Op maten

Wij die op maten als op golven schrijden,
Gedragen door dat open wieglend web,
Wij hebben onder ons de woelge tijden
En boven ons een storend wiekgeklep.

Wij kunnen niet op lichte vleugels glijden
En tussen wolk en straal met klauw en neb
De donkre geesten in hun vlucht bestrijden
Of stijgen waar een lichter volk zich rep.

Wij kunnen enkel zorglijke aandacht wijden
Aan 't mazenweefsel dat ons veilig draagt,
En zingend reizen, godlijke gevrijden,
Naar de Voltooiing, waar ons hart om vraagt.

2   *The voice*

Forgiveness, o forgiveness! cries
The voice that's nothing now but voice.
I seek you, I do want you so
And echo solely answers me.

What is there between me and you
But what you brood on, what I cry:
The guilt of understanding missed,
That moans and broods, that broods and moans

In hollow grave, through hollow vaults
Of empty heavens void of hope.
And then a tremor goes through space
As if in silence you had heard.

3   *On measures*

We who on measures as on waves go striding,
Borne onward by that open yielding web,
We witness under us Time's billows riding,
And over us disturbing pinions clap.

We cannot lightly wing our way and, soaring,
Attack with claw and bill in cloud and beam
The sombre spirits in the welkin warring
Or rise to where the fleeter beings gleam.

We can but concentrate our care on stringing
The web of meshes which our feet require,
And, godlike freemen, go our journey singing
Towards the Achievement which our hearts desire.

4 Lokroep

Uit de onzekerheid van doen en denken,
Uit de strijd,
Uit de vage en onverklaarbre wenken
Van de tijd,

Roep ik u naar de verborgen bronnen
Van 't geluid,
Zeker dat het hart daar de onbegonnen
Zin beduidt.

Daar is klaarheid die wij daadlijk weten,
Daar is kracht.
En geen beeld dat zich met beeld wil meten
Heeft daar macht.

5 Venus en Eneas

Steeg toch niet Anadyómene
Uit de zee?
Uit het schuim geboren
Kwam ze 't licht behoren

En het was háár zoon die Troje vlood,
Dido's dood
Werkte en stedegronding
Aan de Tibermonding,

Zodat nadien nooit het voorbeeld dooft:
Zwaard dat klooft,
Bouw van wereldrijken,
Stroom van bloed en lijken.

4   Call note

From the doubts of action, speculation,
From the strife,
From all vague mysterious intimation
Of this life

Come with me unto the hidden springs of
Rhythmic sound,
Sure that by the heart those origins of
Sense are found.

There's the clarity of instant knowledge,
Power that creates.
And no image over rival image
Dominates.

5   Venus and Aeneas

Rose not though Anadyomene
From the sea?
She from foam was born
Into light of morn

And it was *her* son fled Troy on fire,
Dido's dire
Fate he wrought, and founded
Rome by Tiber rounded,

So that afterwards the pattern stays:
Sword that slays,
World-empires' erection,
Streams of blood, destruction.

6 *Muren en graven*

Ik sta verwonderd om het ware beeld.
Ik weet: Amfions lier deed Thebe rijzen,
Jericho's muren vielen voor de wijzen
Door 't godlijk volk op de bazuin gespeeld.

Zo hebben onze liedren ook de stenen
Bewogen: staat uw stad niet sterk en hoog
Naast mijne? en puinbrok en gestorte boog
Schoort nog een zuil in 't dreigende overlenen.

En liggen aanstonds niet in graf naast graf
Wij beiden, en vernemen in ons duister
De stille stem van éénzelfde gefluister,
Wendende onze aandacht van 't verscheidene af?

7 *Gevonden*

Heb ik gevonden wat ik niet kon vinden:
De zeebries samen met de zoele winden,
De zang die u en mij voorgoed vereent,
De golf waaraan uw lichaam lijnen leent?

Toen ik mijn afscheid van u nam, bevingen
Bij ieder laatste woord mij aarzelingen:
Het vreemde weten van een dieper bond
Waarvoor ik in dat uur geen woorden vond.

Nu is het stil omdat ge zijt gestorven
En in die stilte heb ik het verworven:
Het denken, en het horen, en het zien
Van u geheel, en 't zeggen bovendien.

6 Walls and graves

I marvel as I find the image true.
I know: Amphion's lyre laid Thebes' foundations,
Jericho's walls fell to the incantations
Of God's people when their trumpet blew.

Thus verily did we once by our singing
Move stones: stands not your city strong and high
Next mine? – fane-wall and arch, though crumbling nigh
Stay to a column ominously clinging.

And shall not we anon in our two graves
Be lying, and in rapt attention hearken
To one still voice that whispers in our darkness,
Turning from multifariousness our gaze?

7 Found

Have I now found what I despaired of finding:
The sea-breeze and the mellow winds uniting,
The enduring union of your song and mine,
The wave to which your body lends its line?

As my farewell was said to you, there stirred
In me a doubt at every parting word:
Strange knowledge of a kinship more profound
Which in that final hour no utterance found.

Now it is still because you have departed
And in that stillness to me is imparted
The thinking, and the hearing, and the view
Of yours entire – the very voice of you.

8 *Twee en een*

Laat het zo zijn: door alle tijden strijden
Wij met elkaar.
U zullen de enen ginds een altaar wijden,
Mij de andren daar.

Maar als de rook weerzijdig opwaarts wiegelt,
Rein en alleen,
Worden twee zuilen, door één blauw bespiegeld,
Onscheidbaar één.

Dan zenden twee verbondene gelaten
Eén straal op de aard,
En huivrend vraagt het volk in stad en staten
Wat hun weervaart.

9 *Mijn koning*

Toch kan ik zo niet einden, want
Ik zie u anders dan mijzelf.
Wie trok er ooit zo klare lijn
Om zich als gij, wie wist zich zo

Van andren aftegrenzen? Wie
Verleende al zijn gebaren zulk
Een nadruk? Al zijn woorden zulk
Een glans? Wie wist zijn vorm

Zo inteprenten in een jong
Geslacht? Ik buig mij als ik dit
Bedenk. Vol eerbied fluister ik:
Mijn koning! en ik zwijg en ga.

8   *Two and one*

Let it be so: each through the ages wages
War on the other.
Your shrine shall there by some be consecrated,
Mine here by others.

But as on either side the smoke unfolds
Pure and alone,
Two rival columns which one blue beholds
Merge into one.

Then there descends from two joined countenances
One shaft of rays,
And from the towns and states rise upward glances
Of awed amaze.

9   *My king*

Yet thus I cannot end here, for
I see you different from myself.
Who ever drew so clear a line
Around himself but you, who so

Could mark himself from others? Who
Would lend to all his gestures such
A weight? to every utterance such
A splendour? Who could stamp his form,

Imprint it thus into a young
Generation? At this thought I bow
My head. Awe-struck I whisper: Lo,
My king! and silently I go.

10   Het Andre

Ik ben een Vriend. Ik nam voor mij
Als het mij toegemeten deel
Al wat ik liefhad. Niemand kan
Mij dat ontnemen.

Ik leef in 't Andre en 't Andre in mij.
Ik ben niet in omsloten lijn.
Niet één leeft die mij kennen kan
Zonder het Andre.

Ik buig me en richt mij dan weer op.
Ik weet dat een gezaamheid blijft.
Geen God, geen Wereld, of in mij
Werden zij Andre.

11   Orfeus

Grijze dagen! en begraven
Heb ik hem die in mijn hart leeft.
Vraag ik of er vreugde of smart leeft?
Alles rust in veilge haven.

Zon zal straks de wolken delen
En wat donker ligt zal uitgaan.
Moge een Orfeus maar de luit slaan
En niet omzien bij zijn spelen.

Geen begeren roept de doden
Maar de zang die in zichzelf rust.
Elk die in mijn harts gewelf rust
Zal het lied niet vruchtloos noden.

10   The Other

I am a Friend. I took as mine,
As what was my allotted share
All that I loved. There's no one who
Can take that from me.

I live in the Other, It in me.
I'm not within a line enclosed.
By none that lives can I be known
Without the Other.

I bow down and once more arise.
I know that a joint life abides.
No God, no World, but they in me
Grew to be Other.

11   Orpheus

Grey the days are! and I've buried
Him who yet within my soul lives.
What if therein joy or woe lives?
All in a safe haven tarries.

Sun will part the clouds now weighing,
And what slumbers will from dark spring,
If an Orpheus strike the harp-string
Without glancing back from playing.

Not our yearning calls the dead,
Only song that self-contained rests.
Whoso in my heart enshrined rests
Shall my voice not vainly bid.

12   Het lichtfeest

Zing dan, zang, en roep hem
Luid naar 't aardefeest.
Wij zijn tal van dagen
In 't licht en saamgeweest.

Wij zullen tal van dagen
Saamzijn in het licht,
Of ook mijn lijf als 't zijne
Zijn arbeid heeft verricht.

Ook als mijn lijf als 't zijne
Onder de zoden rust,
Roept ons de zang naar 't feestlicht,
Dat nooit wordt uitgeblust.

25–26 December 1933

Het speeltuig

Vreemde speler, die mij het gebonden
Aan een omloop buiten mijn verstand,
Zodat telkens weer, na veel of weinig ronden,
Al mijn toetsen openliggen voor uw hand,

Buiten u kan geen akkoord verluiden,
Geen akkoord verluidt of 't is alleen
Als een regelrecht vervolg te duiden
Van het voorge en met alle andren één.

Machtloos ben ik, niet alleen tot spreken,
Maar tot schikken, reeglen naar mijn gril.
Nooit kan ik de levenslange rede breken
Die gij eens begont door mij en voortzet naar uw wil.

Onverbidbre! ik dacht u soms te ontkomen,
Vrij te zijn, naar menselijke lust
Her en der te gaan, in doelloos dromen
Te genieten van mijn rust.

12   *The feast of light*

Sing then, song, and call him
Loudly to earth's rite.
We have been together
Through countless days of light.

So shall we be together
Sharing days of sun,
Although like his, my body's
Labour will be done.

And when like his, my body
Rests beneath the grass,
We shall by song be bidden
To a light that quenchless lasts.

The instrument

Strange musician, who hast bound me
To an orbit past my conscious mind,
So that soon or late when Time's revolved around me,
All my keys lie open to thy hand,

Outside thee not one chord can be sounded,
Not a chord will sound but must perforce
As a direct sequel be expounded,
One with all the others in their course.

Powerless am I, and not just to say,
But to order, by caprice or skill.
Never can I break the lifelong lay
Which thou once began through me and further by thy will.

Ruthless one! I sometimes thought to escape thee,
To be free, and, as we humans please
Roaming here and there in aimless dreaming
To enjoy my peace.

Maar ik dwaas, terwijl ik zocht en dwaalde,
En vergeefs, met telkens minder kracht,
Hoopte dat ik zelf mijn spieren staalde,
En onttrok ze uw overmacht,

Kwam uw drift die me als uw snaartuig spande
En een kreet ontging me op 't onvoorzienst,
Daar nog eens uw geest mij overmande, en bande
In uw dienst.

23 April 1934

Aan een vriend die wil dat ik vrede predik

Wat baat het, Vriend, of op mijn zeeduin ik,
De dichter, vrede predik, onderwijl
De volken, aangevoerd door bendehoofden,
Zich van elkaar afzondren, en bekwamen
Tot roof en moord. Ge ziet hoe zelfs de Paus,
Hoofd van een Christenheid, zich schuchter uit
En aan geen vlammende betogen denkt.
Er is nu niet op onze nietige ster,
Eén mensheid die de wondren van 't verkeer
Gebruikt tot voeding van haar honderd leden: –
Die leden zelf zijn groepen, eigenmachtig
Bedacht op 't naaste voordeel, liever hongrend
Dan dat de een de ander 't naakte leven gunt.
Zelf slaven, in de ketens van hun waan,
Hunkrend naar welvaart en gemeenschap, slaan zij
De haken van hun haat naar alle zijden
En worden armer en eenzelviger.
Vrede verkondig ik niet meer. Het heil
Kan enkel komen van een uitgeputte
Wereld, die na haar koorts zich nieuw bezint.
Als straks elk volk, schamel teruggezonken
In eigen machteloosheid, zich bezint
Op 't weten van de weingen dat heroën
Niet zijn de brallende verheerlijkers

Fool I was ! – for, as I searched, meandered
Vainly, and with ever lessening strength,
Hoping I myself might steel my powers,
And escape thy might at length,

Came thy urge that like a harp-string strained me,
And a cry broke from me suddenly,
As once more thy spirit tamed and claimed me
To serve thee.

To a friend who wishes me to preach peace

Of what avail is it, my friend, if I,
The poet, on my seashore dune preach peace,
Whereas the nations, headed by gang-leaders,
Segregate from each other and are training
For robbery and murder. See, how ev'n the Pope,
Head of a Christendom, speaks timidly,
Not venturing to indulge in ardent utterance.
There is not now, upon our puny star,
One humankind using the transport-marvels
So as to nourish all its hundred members:
Those members now are sections, selfishly
Seeking their own advantage, rather starving
Than granting neighbours their bare livelihood.
Slaves as they are, chained by their own delusions,
Longing for welfare and community,
They slash about them with their hooks of hate,
And grow still poorer, more turned inward yet.
It is not peace I urge now any more:
Salvation can but come when an exhausted
World after its fever will recover sense.
When presently each nation, then sunk back
In wretched impotence, takes thought
On what is realised by the few: that heroes
Are not the ranting glorifiers

Van land of natie, maar de stille dragers
Van 't bovenvolkelijk verband, - eerst dan
Komt vrede, niet als een papieren bond,
Verscheurbaar door elk vaderlandse dwaas,
Maar als het net uit diamanten draden
Van de geheiligde Noodzaaklijkheid.
Tot deze bid ik, want elke andre godheid
Is machtloos. Recht is machtloos. Liefde is machtloos.
Gelooft er iemand nog aan recht? Dit is juist
De ervaring van wie langer leefde: Recht
Is overal de sluier van 't belang.
Wij doen, wij leven, maar wij denken nooit
De volle vreeslijkheid ons in, dat niemand
Bestaan kan zonder daaglijks zelf-vervreten,
Dan gekastreerd van rechtsbesef. Wij schuiven
De wereld als een onrechtvaardig iets
Op de achtergrond van ons bewustzijn, zien
Schouderophalend elk bizonder onrecht,
Als of 't een schim was uit de camera
Van een aanvaarde duivel, en gaan verder,
Koud, en geharnast in ontgoocheling.
En Liefde? Een huiselijke zaak, niet wijder
Reikend dan tot gezin en vrienden. Dat zij
Werelden drijft is wel een schone droom.
Maar déze wereld drijft toch eer de Haat.
Zo bid ik dan tot de Noodzaaklijkheid
Dat zij, de volken nopend tot steeds feller
Eigenzucht en verdeeldheid, twist en strijd,
Hen murw maakt tot de Vrede. Nood en wanhoop,
Chaos en waanzin bid ik dat zij uitstort
Over de opstandige onverstandigen,
Die menen dat hun dwaasheid wijsheid is.
Ik predik oorlog, oorlog. Niet omdat –
Naar 't zeggen van krijgshaftige drilfiguren –
Oorlog de man beter en sterker maakt,
Maar omdat de verarming, de verbeesting,
Die zeker volgt, vernedert en bereidt
Voor 't knallen van Uw grote drilzweep, wijze
Goede en rechtvaardige Noodzaaklijkheid.

1935

Of country, nation; but the quiet bearers
Of international solidarity, –
Only then peace will come, not as a paper league,
That can be torn apart by any folk-drunk fool,
But as the net, woven from diamond threads,
Of holy sacrosanct Necessity.
To her I pray, for every other deity
Is powerless: Justice powerless; Love is powerless.
Does anyone believe in justice still?
This is the experience of one longer-lived:
Everywhere Justice is veiled interest.
We act, we live, but never realise
Fully the dreadful fact that no-one can
Exist unless by daily eating out his heart,
Unless castrated of the sense of justice.
We push the world as 'twere an unjust thing
Into the background of our thoughts, we see,
Shrugging our shoulders, each injustice
As if it were a shadow in the slide-show
Of an acknowledged devil, and pass on,
Cold, armoured in our disillusionment.
And Love? A home affair, no further reaching
Than to our families and friends. That she
Moves worlds – it is indeed a beautiful dream,
But *this* world's surely rather moved by Hate.
Therefore I pray unto Necessity
That she, driving the nations to still fiercer
Self-seeking and division, dispute, strife,
May break them in to Peace. I pray that she
May pour out chaos, madness over all
The many senseless and rebellious ones
Who *will* believe their folly to be wise.
I preach war, war. Not indeed because –
According to the warlike drilling-masters –
War makes men into better, stronger beings,
But since impoverishment and beastliness,
Certain to follow, will humiliate and prepare
For the cracking of thy mighty drilling-whip,
Wise, good and righteous Necessity.

Ik ben

Ik heb de tijd gedragen en geleden,
Zo lang, tot ik zijn vingers losmaakte en
Hem vallen liet in 't slijk waar hij wil treden.
Ik red mij niet in een ivoren toren,
Maar in het zachte indringend woord: Ik ben,
Dat woont in allen die mijn woorden horen.
Al zijn 't er weingen die 'k als zulken ken.

En was 't er geen; ook dan nog zou ik 't uiten,
Verzekerd dat een zo gesproken woord
Mijn kwijtbrief is in 't fonds dat niet wil sluiten.
Geen enkle tijd heeft recht de waan te kweken
Dat hij de hele tijd is: hem behoort
Zijn deel, mij 't mijne; en met dit uittespreken
Doe ik naar 't simple recht, dat niemand smoort.

1936

Vernietiger Tijd

Vernietiger Tijd, ik worstel lijf aan lijf
Met u die grof en zwaar en honderdledig
Mij die mij machtloos als een kind verdedig
Knelt in uw slangige armen sterk en stijf.

Geen uitzicht ooit dat ik u ván mij drijf.
Gij gaaft, gij neemt; en zult aanstonds niet ledig
Van hier gaan. Vrolijk dat ik u bevredig
Fluistert ge nu alreê: gij gaat, ik blijf.

Maar als ik dood ben tikt een op uw schouder
En zegt: Nu mij: ik ben hem: want zijn geest.
En dan, misschien, wordt het gemoed u kouder.

'I am'

I have endured the time and I have borne
So long, till I undid his fingers' clam
And dropped him in the slime, where he *will* turn.
I seek no shelter in an ivory tower,
But in the gentle haunting word: 'I am',
Which dwells in all who feel my tranquil power,
Although but few of them I know by name.

And were there none, I'd speak it even then,
Being certain that an utterance spoken thus
Acquits me in the fund that will not close.
Not one time has the right to breed the view
That he's the whole of time: to him is due
His share, as mine's to me; these words I chose
I speak as Justice wills, who smothers none.

Destroyer Time

Destroyer Time, I bodily must fight
You who now, heavy, coarse, limbed manifold
Clench me, who ward off weakly like a child,
Fiercely in your strong arms so tight.

No hope that you will evermore give way.
You gave, you take; and soon will not go void
Of prey from here. Pleased you'll be satisfied,
You're whispering even now: you'll go, I stay.

But when I'm dead, another taps your shoulder
Saying: Me next: I'm him: my spirit is.
And then, maybe, your bold heart will grow colder.

Want hij die is lijkt hem die is geweest
Gelijk een broeder en een evenouder,
En lacht: Na mij eenzelfde, in 't eeuwige feest.

1936

De Dood

Wil nu de Dood niet de Verdelger noemen.
Hij komt en wacht op wat de Tijd hem brengt.
Zijn vrede weet van worstelen noch roemen.

Hij is het niet die ons met koortsgloed zengt,
De spier en zenuw spant en pijn doet lijden.
Hij is het ook niet die de slaapdrank mengt.

Hij is de ontvanger van wie niet meer strijden,
De zachte groeter na de luide kreet:
Hij is de god die meer weet dan de tijden.

Ik ken hem niet als wie op zerken treedt:
Een rammelend geraamt met naakte schonken
Of flardig en paskwillig aangekleed:

De mensenjager met de geile lonken
Die jong en oud, en hoog en laag, en rijk
En arm ten dans vraagt, van verdelging dronken:

Zelf de burleske rest van 't menslijk lijk.
Hem mocht men boven kerkportalen beelden
Of om een kerkhof of als kunstige prijk

In prenteboeken teeknen, waar de weelden
Van verf en zilverstift en scherts en spot –
Macabre fantazie – rondom hem speelden:

For he who was is seen in him who is,
As that young brother, vying with the elder,
Laughs: Soon my like will join life's endless bliss.

Death

No more let Death be the Destroyer called.
He comes and he awaits what Time will send:
Peace-bringer, not vainglorious or bold.

He sends not fever-heat to make us pant,
Nor makes tense nerves and muscles suffer pain,
Nor comes to us the sleeping-draught to blend.

He is the home for those who no more strain,
The gentle welcome after piercing throes,
The god who knows more than the times divine.

I know him not as who on gravestones goes,
A rattling skeleton with naked shank
Or dressed-up, farcical, in ragged clothes:

Hunter of humans who with leering prank
Invites young, old, and proud and lowly, lame
And whole to dance with him, destruction-drunk:

Himself the burlesque relic of man's frame.
He used to be above church doors portrayed,
Or round a churchyard or, as dainty trim

Drawn in illuminated books well-made,
Where grace of paint and stylus, mocking, odd,
– Macabre fantasy – around him played.

Hij is de Dood niet, niet de raadsel-god
Die roerloos is en waterdiep van ogen.
Hij niet de weter van ons grondloos lot.

Hij is niet vreeslijk, niet met ons bewogen.
Hij is ook niet, o neen, de schone knaap,
Die, voeten om elkaar, het hoofd gebogen,

Bij graven staat, als broeder van de Slaap.
Hij is de hoeder van de wereldgrenzen,
De staande wachter op de nevelkaap,

Die zeis noch fakkel hoeft opdat wij mensen
Hem kennen mogen als zijn vorm verrijst.
Wij kennen hem, zodra ons laatste wensen

Ons naar niets meer dan naar onszelf verwijst.
Dan staat hij daar en draagt onze eigen trekken,
Toch vreemd, want groter dan ons hart ze prijst:

Vertrouwlijk, als gereed om ons te ontdekken
Wat onze droom vragende heeft gegist
Van 't land dat aanbreekt achter deze hekken.

Want wij zijn kindren, en met lieve list
Dromen wij ons hierna gezellige weiden
Of vrezen sombre en laaghangende mist:

Hel dreigt en hemel lokt en tussen beiden
Toeft ons de boete in 't reinigende vuur.
De een zint op niet-zijn, d'andre op voorbereiden

Tot omloop in een andre kreatuur
Op aarde, een derde hoopt met ziel en zinnen
Zich te offren aan de heilige Natuur.

Zo onze dromen. En hij laat ons binnen
En loochent niet, maar geeft aan 't levenseind
Altijd de wijding van een nieuw beginnen,

He is not Death, not the mysterious god
Who is all stillness, water-deep his eyes.
He knows not our unfathomable lot.

Death is not frightening, does not feel for us,
Nor is he – no – the fair youth whom we keep
Gladly in mind, head bowed and feet cross-wise,

Who stands by graves, the brother-god of Sleep.
He is the guardian of Earth's borderline,
The watchman standing on the mist-bound cape,

Who needs not scythe nor torch so we divine
And know him as we see his form arise.
We know him when the last wish we retain

Points to our self alone, since all else flies.
Then he stands forth, his traits our own we know,
Yet strange, greater than we at heart surmise:

Inviting, and as if prepared to show
What in our dreams we wonderingly guessed
About the land that lies beyond our view.

For we are children, and with touching zest
We dream of a hereafter meadow-green,
Or we fear sombre and low-hanging mist:

Hell threatens, heaven draws, and in between
Awaits us expiation in the purging fire.
One ponders not-to-be, another would again

Resume the round and be another creature
On earth, a third will hope, with soul and sense
To give his being up to sacred Nature.

Such are our dreams. And he will let us in,
Denying not, but giving to life's close
Always the hallowing of what is to begin,

Omdat als iets verdwijnt ook iets verschijnt.
Hoe hem te beelden? Wind is in zijn haren
Van tocht door de open deur. Zijn oog omlijnt

Een diepe bron, waarin wij dromend staren,
En in zijn hand draagt hij de nenufar,
Die van twee elementen weet: het varen

Op 't water en het reiken naar een star,
En van het spieglen als het ware weten:
Het spiegelraadsel, dat ik niet ontwar.

Is dit dan, Dood, de telkens weer vergeten
Waarheid die ge in onze uiterste uur ons toont:
Dat waarheid slechts in spiegling wordt bezeten:

Dat gij zelfs niet ons van de vraag verschoont
Naar de Verborgenheid van alle dingen
En zien laat waar zij onverborgen woont?

Ge draagt een spiegel aan uw gordel? Gingen
Uw voeten wijd vaneen als van wie staat
Aan weerszij van een drempel, en omringen

Slangen uw polsen, wier gebit zich slaat
Om de eigen staart, opdat we goed beseffen
Dat de eeuwge cirkel nergens ruimte laat

Voor punt waar wij begin en einde treffen?
Verborgenheid die slechts in spiegling leeft,
Voorgoed ons afsluit van elk zelf-verheffen,

En nergens recht op een ontraadsling geeft?
Nu is het, Dood, alsof ik u hoor fluistren:
Er is geen god voor wie het leven heeft

En weer een die van 't leven kan ontkluistren.
Ik ben het Leven en Die leeft is Ik.
Elkanders Andre, lichten we en verduistren.

Because when something goes, a new thing grows.
How to portray him? Wind-blown is his hair
With draught from the open door. His eyes enclose

A deep well, into which we dreaming stare,
And in his hand he bears the nenuphar, ★
Which knows two longings: tranquilly to fare

On water and to reach out towards a star,
And knows of mirroring, true lore to learn:
The mirror-mystery on which I pore.

Is this then, Death, the evermore re-born
Truth which in our ultimate hour you reveal:
That truth is only found in mirrored form:

That you not even let us off the spell
Of Mystery in all things, nor will show
Us plainly where unhidden it may dwell?

You wear a mirror in your girdle? Do
Your feet stand wide apart as though you step
On either side a threshold; are there two

Serpents twined round your wrists that ever snap
Each its own tail, that we may understand
That the eternal circle leaves no gap

For us to find where 't may begin and end?
The mystery that has but mirrored life,
For ever cuts off self-aggrandisement,

And nowhere grants the light towards which we strive?
Now, gently, Death, I seem to hear you say:
There's not *one* god for those who are alive

Another one who can from life set free.
I am the Life, and He – Life – is Myself.
Each, other's Other, shines, and fades away.

★ the water lily

Gij die als Vorm, bewust zijt van uw ik
Kent mij als Leven, en ik zal het blijven
Totdat ge u geeft aan 't vormen-loos Niet-ik.

Dan zal mijn naam uw heengaan onderschrijven:
Ik ben de Dood, uw dood, deze ogenblik.

Biddende jongeling

Hef nu uw handen als een schaal
Waarop ge onzichtbre vlammen draagt,
Jongling die bidt, maar klaagt noch vraagt,
En niet meer poogt naar mensetaal,

Doch enkel uw gestalte spant
Waarin het hart klopt hemelhoog,
Een schone strakgespannen boog
In eveneens onzichtbre hand.

Zo staat ge en zijt het lichaam zelf
Dat van aardmiddelpunt tot zon
't Heelal begeerde, en nu zich won
Als stille spil van zijn gewelf.

1936

De denker

Achter de gordijn van dood en leven,
Waterval die eindloos stort,
Zit de Denker, roerloos, en zijn armen
Sluiten om zijn knieën, maar zijn hoofd
Hangt zwaar.
In zijn borst beweegt de wereld,

You who, as Form, are conscious of your self
Know me as Life, and Life I shall remain
Till you surrender to form–less Non–self.

Then shall my name your going underline:
'Lo, I am Death, your death, this Now itself.'

Praying youth

Now raise your hands as 'twere a bowl
On which you're bearing unseen flames,
O youth who pray, but beg nor plain,
And no more strive for speech at all,

But hold your outstretched body spanned
In which the heart beats heaven–borne,
A lovely bow that's tautly drawn
Held in a likewise unseen hand.

And so you stand, the living form
That from earth's centre to the sun
Desired the universe, and won
Himself as still shaft of its dome.

The thinker

Past the flowing screen of death and life,
Waterfall that ever pours,
Sits the Thinker, moveless, and his arms
Round his knees are folded, but his head
Hangs down.
In his breast the world is moving,

In zijn hart houdt hij gemeenschap
Met de 't Al doorcirklende gedachten.

Dit is – denkt hij – 't laatstgevonden
Machtigste evenwicht: de wereld stromend,
En ik naast haar, en nochtans de wereld
In mijzelf.

Naar 't andre land

Naar 't andre land, mijn Ziel!
Wie wijs zijn weten dat elk lot zich wendt.
Hijs nu het zeil: te lang reeds wiegde aan eendre kust
Uw boot: bevleugeld ijlt
Door vreemde zee naar verre berg het kielhout voort.

Verlost van ambt, niet langer tot het bootsen
Van 't zinnebeeldige gebaar gedoemd,
Zit ik, een naakte –
Als aan de voeten van een eeuwge Vader
De aartsengel Abdiël, uitziend naar 't heelal.

Southey voor Derwentwater

"Eén ogenblik: het meer was stil,
Zó stil dat het geen meer meer scheen,
Geen water en geen windgeril
Maar macht van spiegeling alleen,

Een dubbellandschap, laag en hoog,
Waar klaar en ijl elk ding in stond,
Bewegingloos zelfs wat bewoog:
De schoorsteenrook op de achtergrond.

In his heart he's in communion
With the cosmic all-pervading thoughts.

This - he ponders - is the last-found
Mightiest equipoise: the world is streaming,
And I am aside; and yet the world is
In myself.

Towards th'other land

Towards th'other land, my Soul!
Who's wise knows well that every lot will turn.
Now hoist the sail: too long already on the self-same shore
Your boat was rocking: winged
Through foreign seas towards farthest mountain
   speeds the keel.

Set free from office, and no longer doomed
To mould the token images alone,
I sit, a naked one, -
As at the feet of an eternal Father
The archangel Abdiël, eyes towards the universe.

Southey regarding Derwentwater

"One moment's span: the mere was still,
So still, it seemed a mere no more,
No water and no wind did stir,
But mirror-power alone was there,

A double landscape – down, above,
Where clear and tenuous each thing stood,
Motionless even what did move:
The chimney-smoke that yonder showed.

Het was een bergzoom maar wier lijn
Op eenmaal zonk en dan weer steeg,
En zichtbaar lag een lang ravijn,
En wei, geboomte en huisjes kreeg

Een ongewone helderheid
Van 't middaguur, en spiegling was
Zo één en zonder onderscheid
Met werklijkheid, dat ook het glas

Van 't nat zich niet herkennen liet,
Maar dubble hemel, dubbele aard,
Van voorgrond tot het verst verschiet,
Onscheidbaar één en toch gepaard,

Leek hangen in een wondre sfeer,
Een landschap in een vreemd heelal,
Waarnaar ik staarde en wist niet meer:
Was 't Al een droom of droom het Al.

Een oogwenk maar: een koeltje ontspant,
Een rimpling breekt de rust van 't beeld:
Ik zie het meer, ik zie het land,
En de Afgrond, hoog en laag, gedeeld."

12 July 1912

Delfse Vermeer, ziende naar Delft zoals hij het zal schilderen

"Een stad aan de overkant,
Met torens, poorten, daken,
Walschoeiingen en aken,
Wolkschaduw, zonnebrand.

Wij zien van de overzij
Het voegschrift in haar muren,
Haar koele kleurglazuren,
Haar verte en haar nabij.

There was a mountain-ridge whose line
Abruptly sank, then to ascend,
And, plainly seen, a long ravine,
And meadow, trees and cottage gained

A brightness, an uncommon light
From mid-day's hour: reflection was
So wholly an unbroken sight
With the reality – the glass

Of water was not recognised,
But double heaven, double earth,
From foreground to the farthest rise,
Uncleavable yet twofold both,

Seemed hanging in a wondrous sphere,
A world under so strange a spell,
That as I gazed I knew no more
If all was dream, or dream the All.

One moment's pause: a waft of air,
A rippling makes the still shapes flow:
I see the mere, I see the shore;
The Deep divides: on high – below."

Vermeer seeing Delft as he will paint it

"A town on yonder side,
With towers and roofs and gateways,
Embankment and long barges,
Cloud-shadow, sunny light.

From here we can descry
The joint-marks in her buildings,
The cool glaze of her colours,
Things distant and near by.

Hoe overtreft haar glans
Haar spiegelschijn in 't water! –
Straalt zo de Godsstad later
Tot schijn mijn stad van thans?"

How far she does outshine
Her image in the water! –
Will so God's City later
Outshine this town of mine?"

Bibliography

Abercrombie, Lascelles, *The Art of Wordsworth* (London, 1952).
Aler, Jan, *Symbol und Verkündung – Studien um Stefan George* (Heidelberg, 1976)
Baker,James V., *The Sacred River: Coleridge's theory of the imagination* (Louisiana, 1957).
Baxter, B.M., *Albert Verwey's translations from Shelley's Poetical Works* (Leiden, 1965)
Boehringer, Robert, *Mein Bild von Stefan George* (Munich–Düsseldorf, 1951).
George, Stefan, *Werke* I, II (Munich–Düsseldorf, 1958).
—, *Zeitgenössische Dichter* I (included in *Werke* II).
Jäckle, Erwin, *Rudolf Pannwitz und Albert Verwey im Briefwechsel* (Zurich, 1976).
Jones, John, *The Egotistical Sublime: a history of Wordsworth's imagination* (Oxford, 1962).
Legouis, Emile, *La jeunesse de Wordsworth, 1770–98: Étude sur 'Le Prelude'* (Lyons, 1896).
Nijland-Verwey, Mea, *Albert Verwey en Stefan George: De documenten van hun vriendschap* (Amsterdam, 1965).
—, *Wolfskehl und Verwey: Die Dokumente ihrer Freundschaft* (Heidelberg, 1968).
Pannwitz, Rudolf, *Albert Verwey: Ausgewählte Gedichte übertragen von R. P.* (Munich–Feldafing, 1933).
— *Albert Verwey und Stefan George: Zu Verwey's hundertstem Geburtstag* (Heidelberg–Darmstadt, 1965).
Rader, Melvin, *Wordsworth: A philosophical approach* (Oxford, 1967).
Salin, Edgar, *Um Stefan George* (Munich–Düsseldorf, 1954).
Uyldert, Maurits, *Uit het leven van Albert Verwey: I De jeugd van een dichter* (1948); *II Dichterlijke strijdbaarheid* (1955); *III Naar de Voltooiing* (1959).
Verwey, Albert, *Oorspronkelijk Dichtwerk* I, II (Amsterdam, 1938).
— *Proza I-X* Amsterdam, 1921-3).
— *Dichtspel: Oorspronkelijke en vertaalde gedichten*, ed. Dr Mea Nijland-Verwey (Amsterdam, 1983).
— 'Het kader van mijn levenswerk' (posthumous), ed. Maurits Uyldert, *Tijdschrift voor Nederlandse Taal- en Letterkunde* XLIV (1954), pp. 232 ff.

Vestdijk, S., *Albert Verwey en de Idee* (Rijswijk, 1940; photostat reprint, 1965.

Weevers, Theodoor, 'Albert Verwey's ultimate understanding of Stefan George', *Modern Language Review*, XLIX, 1954, pp. 129–55.

— *Poetry of the Netherlands in its European context, 1170–1930* (London, 1960).

— *Mythe en Vorm in de gedichten van Albert Verwey* (Zwolle, 1965).

— *Droom en Beeld – De Poëzie van Albert Verwey* (Amsterdam, 1978).

Wolf, Manfred, *Albert Verwey and English Romanticism* (The Hague, 1977).

Notes

I Introduction

1 *Oorspronkelijk Dichtwerk* (henceforth abbreviated *OD* I or II), II, p. 502.

II Albert Verwey in his time – a short biography

1 This chapter is mainly based on the biography by Maurits Uyldert, *Uit het leven van Albert Verwey*, vols. I,II,III, to which I refer or which I tacitly follow in Part I.
2 *OD* I, pp. 35–54.
3 *OD* I, pp. 11–18.
4 From ' "Dünenhaus" – An Albert und Kitty Verwey', the second of George's *Lieder von Traum und Tod*. It could be translated like this:

Is there one roof yet that, deeply peaceful,
Free and proud and of such fulness
Drew and held the darkly brooding
Stubborn guest, and would so often
Beckon from afar?

The poem as a whole is a wonderful evocation of that hospitable home.

III Vocation: the idea of poet-hood

1 'Het Dubbelzijdige Schild'. *OD* II, pp. 211 ff.
2 Boris Pasternak, *Safe Conduct*, p. 81, *Boris Pasternak, The collected Prose Works,* arranged with an introduction by Stefan Schimanski, translated by Beatrice Victoria Scott (London, 1945).
3 *OD* II, pp. 308 ff.
4 R. M. Rilke, *Briefe an einen jungen Dichter* (Leipzig, 1929), *p.20.*
5 *Mijn Verhouding tot Stefan George*, quoted from *Albert Verwey en Stefan George,* ed. Mea Nijland-Verwey (Amsterdam, 1965), p. 260.
6 *OD* II, p. 476.

7 'De Levende', *OD* I, p. 501.
8 C.S. Lewis, *An Experiment in Criticism* (Cambridge, 1961), pp. 40–49.
9 Dante, in the lyric beginning: 'I' mi son pargoletta bella e nova'.
   Verwey translates (with one important alteration) the lines:
        Le mie bellezze sono al mondo nove
        Però che di la su mi son venute.
   Verwey deliberately alters 'di la su' ('from on high') and writes:
   'Neen, ik zoek u *niet daar boven*'.
10 Otto zur Linde, *Gesammelte Werke,* Band IV, *Charontischer Mythus* (1910-13) pp.19-21.

IV Organic structure

1 The three titles quoted here form the component parts of the volume *Het Zichtbaar Geheim* (The Visible Mystery) 'The Personal Realm', 'The Realm in the World', 'New Year Morning'.
2 From a posthumous publication edited by Mea Nijland-Verwey, 'Mijn dichterlijk levensbedrijf' in *De Nieuwe Taalgids*, XLIV (1950), pp. 65-74.

V Verwey and Wordsworth: the growth of the poetic imagination

1 *Van Jacques Perk tot nu.* Reprinted in *Albert Verwey. Keuze uit het proza van zijn hoogleraarstijd (1925–1935),* ed. Dr Mea Nijland-Verwey, Zwolle, 1956, pp.12–33.
2 See: *Volkslieder der Serben,* metrisch übersetzt und historisch eingeleitet von Talvj, Leipzig, 1853, p. 78, *Die Erbauung Skadars.* Dr Nijland-Verwey informed me that the poet's attention was drawn to this poem by a relative, the French ethnologist Arnold van Gennep.
3 Homer, *Odyssey,* Book XI, 11. 96–9.
4 *Albert Verwey en de Idee,* pp. 198–9.
5 The poem unmistakably refers to Vondel's dedicatory preface to *Peter en Pauwels,* which contains the lines: 'Eusebia, laat los. Gij trekt my neder, /Die reede al uit den damp der weerelt was' (Eusebia, you drag me down – me already away from the mist of the world) (W.B. edition, IV, 223).
6 Virgil, *Aeneid,* Book VI, 748–51.
7 This line is found only in the early version of 1805.
8 Wordsworth, *The Prelude,* Book XIV, 86 ff. Verwey's

sketches are preserved in the Verwey-Archief in the Amsterdam University Library.

9 This notion of inner conflict likewise links up with *The Prelude*, where 'a twofold frame of body and of mind' is caused by 'that false secondary power by which we multiply distinctions', as it breaks our sense of 'the unity of all'.

10 In the one extant fragment of the planned book on Wordsworth's *poetry* as distinct from *The Prelude*, which is quoted in full in my *Droom en Beeld*, pp.186–196.

11 From 'Gedachten rondom een huis op Goeree', *OD* II p. 308–311.

VI *Verwey and Stefan George: their conflicting affinities*

1 *Mijn Verhouding tot Stefan George*, quoted from Mea Nijland-Verwey, *Albert Verwey en Stefan George*, p. 219.

2 'Albert Verwey en Stefan George – Hun Vriendschap – het keerpunt', *Duitse Kroniek*, XVIII, no. 1/2 (1966), p.48. 'It is then necessary to define the other poet's position as the opposite of what one is oneself, both in one's own opinion and as one wishes to appear in one's work.' See also Aler, *Symbol und Verkündung* (1976) pp. 155–213.

3 As quoted by Aler from Valéry. *Oeuvres*, I (1957–60), p. 600. 'In the creative sphere, which is also the sphere of pride, the necessity of distinguishing oneself from others is inseparable from life itself.'

4 From the 'Songs of Ultimate Understanding', the poem 'Found' (see Part II, p.231 ff.). A commentary on these poems was published by me in *The Modern Language Review,*, XLIX (1954), pp. 129–55, entitled 'Albert Verwey's ultimate understanding of Stefan George'.

5 R. Boehringer, *Ewiger Augenblick*, Aarau, 1945, p.38. Quoted by Dr Mea Nijland-Verwey on p. 198, where she mentions (note 2) an almost identical conversation (January 1929, at Kiel) recorded by Edith Landmann in her *Gespräche mit Stefan George* (1963), p. 195, in which Verwey was mentioned by name.

6 Published by Dr Mea Nijland-Verwey in the above-mentioned book on p. 209; she states that this is an undated and till then unprinted sketch (almost devoid of punctuation) written on a postcard. English rendering:
My poor king, I love you so ...
Because you cannot before anyone
Humble yourself, nor ever can diminish
At all the regal bearing once assumed,

All those desert you who, unlike me, fail
To see your weakness with your greatness. No one knows
How deeply *child* you are, how helplessly
Imprisoned in your self-fostered delusion
Of unhumiliable majesty ...

7　See Part II, pp.174–81
8　See Part II, p.179
9　Stefan George, *Werke* I, p. 370. The initial line of the poem quoted, which occurs in *Der Stern des Bundes,* II, 2, is 'Entbinde mich vom leichten eingangsworte'.
10　*OD* II, p.103. English rendering:

Art thou not seen through human countenances,
Beloved Master, as a re-born face
Transfiguring the former? And the features
Through which dreamlike thy being is revealed
Are they not dear unto our heart as dawn
Is to those longing for the sun's arising?

11　'Kunfttag', I, *Der Siebente Ring*, Gesamtausgabe VI/VII, p.96.
12　See Part II, pp.141–2
13　R. Boehringer, *Mein Bild von Stefan George*, pp. 116–17; discussed by J. Aler, op. cit., pp.39–41.
14　George, *Der Stern des Bundes*, II, 21; Gesamtausgabe VIII, p.70.
15　From the poem 'In de ledige stad' (In the Empty City), *OD* II, pp. 407–8. English rendering:

I knew a friend whose constant prayer was
That a god might come to him. His thinking fostered
The god, his nature, his appearance, till
He even expressed them; – then the god appeared.
Reality, though by himself created,
Or merely seen? – In every thing lie dormant
Potentialities, they're countless, and our eyes
Bring forth into the world what's moved our heart.
I too prayed for a god to come, for a complete
Life, enclosed all round, proportionate
In all its parts, wholly outside myself.
...
My god came not as I had dreamt him. Deep
From out of my sublimest life he trod
Forth in his radiant perfection, and he took
Away my vision of all else...

16　As in 'The Deliverance' and in 'If he were not...' See *OD* I, 804–5 and II, 125.

17 George, *Das Neue Reich, Werke* I, p.466.
18 *OD* II, p. 463, English rendering:
Then I was young, and now I'm old.
How trifling is the difference.
The month, the season are the same,
And I sit here communing still
With them and with my dreams.
...
Whereas my thoughts have still remained
Equally steady, and as vague:
Surmisings by words disciplined,
Yet each one an unfathomed find.

19 English version:
How strange that thoughts should take their course,
Be uttered in entirety,
While yet their sense, plainly expressed,
Proves different and still should tend
Towards knowledge yet unmystified
And never fathomed by the mind.
...
It cannot be. Upon the screen
Of your imagination, I
Draw shadows which that burning fire
Casts through me such that they are seen,
Me who seek fire in shades in vain,
Eternal in a moments' span.

The forms which my eternal light
Captured from time's vicissitude
I gave to you, and gave enough.
I know mine was no shadow-chase,
But on no living eye the sun
Will ever cast his unveiled rays.

20 As was observed by Pannwitz in *Albert Verwey and Stefan George*, p. 28.
21 See Part II, p. 159.
22 *Der Siebente Ring*, Gesamtausgabe I, p. 311.
23 'Wij Beiden', *OD* I, p. 593. Translation: 'We both have the breath that models the word, so that form grows out of sound', i.e.: When our words are spoken, our breath makes their rhythm evocative.
24 I use this term for the short lines of a varying number of syllables

which are spoken naturally in one breath.
25   See Part II, p. 178.
26   George, *Der Stern des Bundes*, III, 1. *Werke*, I, p. 382.
27   *OD* I, p.533, freely paraphrased in English:
Do you not see, my soul? The trees are glowing,
Fields are full of flowers under the sun,
Rivulets springing up as if a bung
Slipped from a full cask; dewy stand the roses.
Among them birds are singing and loving,
– O that like them we could love and sing –
And as if eternal dawn had now begun
The sounds of the world arise and grow silent.

See who are coming! Human forms, erect,
In stature fairer than our earth has seen.
How great and free their glance; upon his hand he shows
A fruit, she leads a lamb; but the wild creatures
Follow them quietly through those fair regions,
Attending meekly to their regal eyes.

28   George, *Der Stern des Bundes*, II, 8. *Werke*, I, p. 309.
29   *OD* II, p. 376.
30   *OD* II, p. 207;
Hij kende aan 't schijnsel van uw hoge lamp
Het licht dat bij beminde en onbevreesd
Wierp hij zich te uwaarts, liet zich neer, omzwermde
Met mateloze en moedige vleugeldrift
Uw stille stralen....
31   George, *Das neue Reich*, (1928) p. 136 and *Werke* I, p. 468.
32   See Part II, p. 237.

VII   *The Universe, a vision of man*

1   Verwey does not seem to have visited the Lake District; no
such trip is mentioned in Uyldert's biography.
2   The original is included in Part II, pp. 258–9.
3   *OD* II, pp. 493–5.
4   *OD* II, pp. 167–71.

Index of persons mentioned in Part I

Index of first lines in Dutch

Index of first lines in English